THE ART OF PARTNERING

How to Increase Your Profits and
Enjoyment in Business Through
Alliance Relationships

Edwin Richard Rigsbee

KENDALL/HUNT PUBLISHING COMPANY
4050 Westmark Drive   Dubuque, Iowa 52002

This edition was printed directly from camera-ready copy.

Printed in the United States of America
10 9 8 7 6 5 4 3 2 1

Dedicated to my wife and partner in life, Regina

ACKNOWLEDGEMENTS

I would like to extend my thanks and sincere appreciation to a number of people with whom I partnered to make this book possible.

—To my wife, Regina, for her love, caring, support, understanding, and encouragement, not only on this project, but throughout our entire twenty-year marriage. Regina, thank you for making do with an absentee husband during the many weeks prior, to this book's completion.

-To our sons, Ryan and Jonathan for their unconditional love, energy, sense of wonder and also, for their tolerance in not seeing much of Dad in these last few months.

—To Robert B. Tucker, Terry L. Paulson, and Dan Poynter, colleagues, mentors, and friends—without whom this book would never have become a reality. These men freely gave many hours of their time to assist me—in everything from idea inception to nurturing, clarity of concept, and manuscript reading and strengthening.

—To the many gracious people who allowed me to tour their businesses, freely giving their time and thoughts.

—To my colleagues and friends who have read the manuscript, and challenged me to do better. Their recommendations strengthened and simplified this project. My sincere appreciation to: Ali Abdel-Haq, Marc Bachrach, Naomi Finkel, Dan Furgang, Mike Geiger, Steve Gordon, Bob Klope, Robert Mecham, Paul Mooney, Rudy Pacal, George Pappas, Rachelle Rolshoven, and Jack Rux.

—Special thanks to Carl F. Frost for phone discussions and supplying me with information that otherwise would have been nearly impossible to obtain. Also to Peter Jeff at Steelcase for his support that was above and beyond the call of duty and his additional assistance in research.

-To Lisa Watson for the countless hours of transcribing my recorded interviews. What a job!

-Additional thanks to Dan Furgang for developing the star graphics at a moments notice, and being available to assist, simply for the asking.

-To Lori Larson, my copy-editor, Sheri Hosek, my production manager, and all the folks at Kendall/Hunt—thanks a million.

Table of Contents

"Synergy means behavior of whole systems unpredicted by the behavior of their parts." -R.[ichard] Buckminster Fuller, *What I have Learned, How little I know* (1966)

"Lofty words cannot construct an alliance or maintain it; only concrete deeds can do that." -John F. Kennedy, address, Frankfurt, Germany, June 25, 1963

"One man may hit the mark, another blunder; but heed not these distinctions. Only from the alliance of the one, working with and through the other, are great things born." -Saint-Exupery, *The Wisdom of the Sands* (1948)

"The highest and best form of efficiency is the spontaneous cooperation of a free people." -Woodrow Wilson (1921)

"Thunder is good, thunder is impressive; but it is lightning that does the work." -Mark Twain (Samuel Langhorne Clemens), Letter to an unidentified person (1908)

"Herein lies the tragedy of the age: not that men are poor,-all men know something of poverty; not that men are wicked,-who is good? not that men are ignorant-what is truth? Nay, but that men know so little of men." -W.E.B. Du Bouis, *The Souls of Black Folk* (1903)

"To crush, to annihilate a man utterly, to inflict on him the most terrible of punishments so that the most ferocious murderer would shudder at it and dread it beforehand, one need only give him work of an absolutely, completely useless and irrational character." -Dostoevsky, *The House of the Dead* (1862)

"We must hang together, or assuredly we shall all hang separately." -Benjamin Franklin, at the signing of the Declaration of Independence, July 4, 1776

INTRODUCTION:

My goal for this book is to give you the insights and tools necessary for you to make partnering a part of your life. *The Art of Partnering* will concentrate on the practical as well as theoretical applications of partnering. So what is partnering? Partnering is *the process of two or more entities coming together for the purpose of developing synergistic solutions to their challenges.*

- Synergistic alliances with other firms creates an environment for collaboration and innovation, that will surpass current industry leaders.
- Partnering with employees will result in an empowered workforce, who are able to discover cost-cutting measures and methods for productivity increases.
- Increase market share by making available additional products or services into your current offering, increase sales, and profits.

Partnering is today's business strategy for long-term success. Partnering is not, nor is it meant to be, a quick fix for your business ills. Even though many of the ideas will provide short-term benefits, the partnering philosophy is not *instant gratification*; it's rather a long-term business strategy that provides synergistic solutions to core needs. Examples of this will be evident as you read the book.

As you explore these pages I'll offer you many opportunities to see and choose new possibilities for your career and your business, no matter what business you are in or position you hold. In these uncertain times everybody, including your competition, is looking for answers—you and your competition alike. This book will enlighten you to the ways of working with others for synergistic (the whole equaling more than the sum of the parts, $1+1=3$) solutions.

Business trends in American manufacturing early in the Twentieth Century, created an era characterized by world dominance. Names like John D. Rockefeller and Andrew Carnegie, became synonymous with integrated conglomerates—they owned it all from natural resources to their distribution.

Today the business trends are corporate divestiture, re-engineering, downsizing, and an overall flattening of the corporate structure. These are the trends that will transport business into the Twenty-first Century, and will continue well into the next century.

For today's cutting-edge business leaders, partnering is the prevailing answer. The Partnering Pentad (my model of building a partnering group of five elements), will enable businesses of any size to access the benefits generated by pooling the knowledge and experience, crucial to compete in the global marketplace.

Partnering is the answer if you are willing to adopt the paradigm of collaboration for mutual success! Challenge yourself not only to read, but to put into action the innovative ideas, solutions and philosophies that will follow.

ONE

THE VALUE OF PARTNERING

My first real job, out of college was in Yosemite National Park working as a retail manager of a sports shop. Work was unsettling because, no one in the company seemed to get along, despite living in one of the most serene and beautiful locations in the country. The operating belief, or paradigm, of this small town company was: "The only way to get ahead was by stepping on somebody else." I couldn't handle it, and left the park after less than a year.

My next job was with a sunglass importer. This company also operated from the position that to win, another must lose. They would speak of doing business as if they were planning strategies for a war. I'd frequently hear, "If you make the sale, you win—if you don't, they win." This never squared with me and many times, early in my career, I would be depressed by the attitude of those for whom I worked. The lessons I learned in that brief span of time will last my lifetime.

It was later in my career when I began experiencing some successes, that I realized I was most successful with people who appreciated the extra service I would deliver. People with whom I had built a relationship. I realized back then, but could not articulate, the belief that when I partnered with customers—treating them as if I had a stake in their business—we both prospered. After a period of time, most of my independent customers would give me carte blanche—allowing me to order for them what I believed was necessary—rarely ever bothering to even sign an order. Even my corporate customers would give me

1

signed blank purchase orders—they knew I wouldn't take advantage of their trust.

This paradigm, or belief system of cooperation was an amazing discovery for me because I frequently thought of myself as being odd for wanting my customers to do well. At that time, just about all of the sales reps I knew couldn't care less about their customers. Their only concerns were getting the order, even if it meant overloading customers with product. In fact a popular saying in my company was, "With 50 dozen in the back, they can't buy from Jack!" (50 dozen was a two year supply for many stores!).

My success in building relationships lead me to eventually become a vice president of the company. Still, their paradigm was that of warfare. As I studied business and successful people, I believed more strongly that even if I was odd for also wanting my customers to win, it was okay, because, I was on the crest of a wave that was sure to change the way America did business. I left my corporate position for what I passionately cared about—helping others. I became a business writer, consultant, and speaker. Allowing me even more involvement in this incredible paradigm of partnering.

Partnering is the best and most powerful long-term strategy for business success. Based on relationship building, partnering will assist you in getting yourself where you want to go without the trail of garbage that follows behind those embracing the old paradigm.

IT BEGINS IN THE MIND

Partnering begins in the mind of an individual. Partnering is germinated by the idea of joining efforts with another to create more for each: *The process of two or more entities coming together for the purpose of developing synergistic solutions to their challenges.* This notion of synergy/mutuality is a core value in creating and maintaining relationships. The basic underpinning in all partnering associations.

Partnering is both an activity and a mindset. Napoleon Hill, began his classic book, *Think & Grow Rich* with a story about a man who "thought" his way into a synergistic alliance with Thomas A. Edison. The man, Edwin C. Barnes, was armed with the chief characteristic of a definite desire to work with Edison as a partner, not *for* him. I believe like Barnes, you can think yourself into successful partnering relationships as long as you are committed to taking definite action—a partnering strategy. When the desire (or impulse of thought) first flashed into his mind, Barnes was not in a position to act on it. When the desire to partner strikes, you too may be faced with a similar challenge.

But he had two difficulties standing in his way: First, he did not know Edison. Second, he didn't have enough money to pay the railroad fare to Orange, New Jersey. Despite these difficulties Barnes found a way to present himself at Mr. Edison's laboratory and announce that he wanted to go into business with the great inventor. About this first meeting Edison said, "I had learned, from years of experience with men, that when a man really desires a thing so deeply that he is willing to stake his entire future on a single turn of the wheel in order to get it, he is sure to win." If you are willing to make this kind of commitment to partnering, surely you'll succeed.

Edison said that it wasn't the man's appearance, as he appeared to be a tramp but "...something in the expression of his face which conveyed the impression that he was determined to get what he had come after." Edison started Barnes at a very nominal wage. Barnes had not yet received the partnership he sought. Edison, the brilliant man that he was, already knew one of the key tenants of successful partnering: Know your partner.

Over the months Barnes' mind was focused on his goal and intensifying his desire to become Edison's business partner. He understood that relationships take time. Unfortunately, in today's hyper-paced world, people often believe that solutions come in the space of a 60 second television commercial. After all, aren't all the solutions to your problems presented in this time format? Sometimes solutions are presented even quicker—in 30 seconds. Barnes' opportunity did come, although not exactly as he expected, and it was met by a prepared Edwin Barnes.

Barnes' opportunity arrived in the form of an office device, known at the time as the Edison Dictating Machine. Barnes saw his opportunity—he knew he could sell the machine and told Edison so. Edison's salesmen were not enthusiastic. He did sell the machine, so successfully that Edison gave him a contract to distribute and market it all over the nation.

To successfully partner, you must follow the steps I'll describe in this book. This means being clear on what you want out of a partnering alliance and who your best candidates might be. Then go after those candidates with the same passion Barnes had for a partnership with Edison. Listed below are four examples of partnering in action.

Financial Network Investment Corporation (FNIC), with 1,700 national representatives, is located in Torrance, California and is one of the largest independent securities broker/dealers in the United States. Recognized by the *Los Angeles Business Journal* in 1992 as, "The largest brokerage house in Los Angeles." President and CEO, Miles Gordon believes that relationships are crucial to business success. He says, "Every morning you wake up and that's all you really own, the relationship. Everything we have is relationship built. We have nothing else. Theoretically, our firm could be out of business everyday. As you wake up, everybody else could have gone to another firm. We have no tangible hard assets other than some cash in the bank."[1]

The Minnesota Connection started in the early 1980s, is an alliance between six direct mail specialists in Minnesota: ACI Telemarketing, Plastic Products, Nahan Printing, Mackay Envelope (owned by Harvey Mackay, author of *Swim With the Sharks* and *Sharkproof*), Gage Lettershop Services, and I.C. System, each source offering only one component in an overall program. The advantages they offer to the industry they serve flow from years of experience working together in a particular style. Each one keeps the other posted on projects so the customer is continually informed as to progress, and because of their close proximity to each other the work gets done faster by eliminating postage and shipping challenges. The advantages for the six are decreased marketing costs, increased flow of work, higher quality through cooperation, and decreased expenses overall. Scott T. Johnson, Vice President, Sales and Marketing for Mackay envelope conveyed, "If we're going to pitch this [the consortium idea], we all have to work at a higher level—function as one company—we can't let anybody down."[2]

United Airlines is partnering at 30,000 feet with McDonald's in an exclusive alliance to offer younger passengers a McDonald's kids meal alternative. United has hopes of expanding this limited test program, to all North American airports. Some attendants are even wearing badges that promote McDonald's on flights where the meals are available. Kurt Lackner, worldwide director of food and beverages for United boasts, "It's something we can do for our customers that the other guys can't."[3]

Corning, in Corning, New York, has 22 alliance ventures in 12 countries as of 1992. Earning contributions from equity alliances accounted for 35% of Corning's net income in 1991. Since its earliest alliance of making cardboard boxes with Charles Rohm Co. in 1924, Corning has been involved in close to 50 joint ventures. Corning Vice Chairman Van Campbell explains that entering into alliances is a decades-old culture, one of collaboration. Campbell states, "We don't view joint ventures as 'one-of' situations like many companies. We view them as an essential way of doing business." Additionally, Campbell declares, "We regard every company in any related industry as a potential partner."[4]

TWO PARTNERING PARADIGMS

There are two paradigms which embrace partnering. The first approach we'll call *Cotton Candy Partnering*. It looks good, tastes good, but is mostly fluff and dissolves into nothing when put it in your mouth. Like cotton candy, this type of partnering has very little substance. Maybe you've seen this sort of partnering. Many talk a good talk but unfortunately few, actually have substance when it comes to implementing the commitments of their partnering dialogue.

The second approach is what I call *Integrity Partnering*. This type of partnering is currently embraced by innovative leaders in a wide array of industries all over the world, and is clearly on the increase. Someone who partners with integrity is the kind of person who continually seeks superior approaches to make their business or company even more successful. "Can't put frosting on a cake made of manure!"[5] says Roger Tompkins, Vice President-California for State Farm Insurance Companies. State Farm is the largest insurer of auto and homeowner's policies in the U.S., with premiums earnings in 1990 at almost $26 billion.[6] Tompkins believes that integrity and responsibility forms the basis of successful partnering.

For the practitioner of Integrity Partnering, synergy is a force for action. This is because partnering, in addition to being an activity, is also a mind-set. This mind-set, is best viewed as a paradigm, one that will deliver many benefits if integrated into your business operations. As you adopt partnering, successful synergistic alliances will become your hallmark.

Synergism is the feature of partnering that generates the benefits you seek. Partnering synergism, though it takes some work at the outset, is what is going to make your life happier, healthier, and more fulfilling through the satisfaction of doing more than you thought possible. This is what the construction industry has discovered. To illustrate this, a recent California legal briefs' article, published by the Associated General Contractors of America-California, stated that partnering is used by Caltrans, the Corps of Engineers, Washington State and Arizona State Departments of Transportation, and BART (San Francisco/Bay Area Public Transportation). The following have expressed interest in the concept: Bureau of Reclamation, Oakland, Sacramento, Contra Costa Public Works, East Bay MUD, Port of Oakland, Santa Cruz County Public Works, Unocal, Granite Construction, Bechtel, Black & Veatch, Dillingham, Hensel Phelps, Lockeed Missile/Space Systems, O'Brien-Kreitzberg, and Teichert.

WHAT IS PARTNERING?

Partnering could, but does not necessarily equate to partnership. While a partnership is contractual, a partnering activity might simply mean working together to build a product— similar to a barn raising of the last century, where the community would come together to assist an individual. The key distinction between partnership and partnering is that in partnering a formal, written agreement isn't always necessary. As I stated earlier, partnering is a paradigm or belief, a successful method to live one's life or behavior for conducting business.

In an age of cut-throat global competition, *trust* allows this new spirit of cooperation, which is afloat in today's businesses from the time honored hand shake relationships to the more formal multi-million/billion dollar contractual agreements. Even with a contract, those who operate from an adversarial paradigm or belief, find that the enforcement of their coveted contract can be more costly than the value of the contract.

Because of this, the decade of the 1990s is fashioning partnering alliances and joint ventures, which are becoming increasingly popular, especially as substitutes for partnerships, mergers and acquisitions. An excellent example of this was the historic, 1991 alliance between IBM and Apple Computer to establish two joint venture companies and the plan to extensively share technologies.

The basic differences separating partnering alliances and joint ventures from the others are that, first, in an alliance, both companies retain their independence as each preserves their structure, culture and chain of command. In contrast, the others would result in a blending, creating a new and different business entity. Second, in an alliance, businesses cooperate on a limited basis—pooling only the resources necessary, usually their core competencies, to synergistically confront a specific situation, product, or market.

Miles Gordon, CEO at Financial Investment Network, states his philosophy about the people he partners with. They are, "People that you want to do business with because it is a mutually advantageous, win/win position. Whether that be other employees, other representatives, other suppliers or other persons that are tangentially related to our business—lawyers, accountants, people like that."[7]

Roger B. Tompkins defines partnering as, "A relationship which occurs when two or more people voluntarily commit to help each other as part of achieving what each wants to achieve, independently." This is accomplished through partnering elements, of the many elements necessary, Tompkins recommends:

- The sense of a "circle of interests," arising out of his/her own goals.
- The knowledge of the "circle of interests" of another person which he/she perceives to overlap his/her own circle.
- A voluntary effort to work together to seek ways to accomplish both sets of goals.[8]

If you view partnering activities as being at some place on a partnering continuum, and that various partnering activities and relationships might be more representative of a rainbow of colors, rather than being black or white, you will begin to recognize the many possibilities. "If you want a simplistic answer [about partnering], a vendor is somebody who makes something to their specifications and sells them to whomever," declares Jim Rutherford, manager of marketing communications at Steelcase. "A strategic alliance is somebody that you're taking advantage of their strengths and they're taking advantage of your strengths. But it's still an arms length transaction. A partner is where you're working together to provide value to a common customer."[9]

REASONS FOR PARTNERING

The reasons become apparent when you, regardless of your company size, understand the benefits of entering into synergistic alliances. Whether the alliances are for research, production, marketing, distribution, and management—your increased capability for success through partnering will encourage your adopting the practice. The same holds true regardless of entering partnering alliances as an individual or organization. Some reasons are:

• To receive a technological contribution or possibly a technological edge in your industry like the alliance between IBM and Apple to develop a new computer operating that allows both hardware formats to communicate, or like Nynex Corp. and Philips Electronics who joined to develop screen telephones for residential use.

• Additional business to justify operating a production facility.

• Access to new markets both domestic and international. Copeland Corporation joined with the largest compressor manufacturer in India, Kirloskar, to bring air conditioning to a growing middle class.

• To differentiate one's self from the competition. Steelcase's alliance with Peerless Lighting, located in Berkeley, California, to offer state-of-the-art office lighting has done just that. "I estimated that this lighting system could bring Steelcase anywhere from $15 to $35 million in additional furniture sales [yearly] just because we have it," suggests Steve Eldersveld, marketing, architectural products at Steelcase.[10] This is extra furniture business, not including the additional dollars received from the light fixture billings.

• Partnering in a poor economy or recession makes good sense especially, when sales are flat and prices are deflating. Continental Airlines is accessing optical industry consumers by partnering with Swan Optical, Inc., an industry supplier, to increase business through a air travel discount certificate program for purchasers of optical frames supplied by Swan.

• Competition from non-traditional sources—through partnering. You can be the creator. Bank of America is locating branch offices in suburban supermarkets and are making consumer lives easier by reducing the amount of their daily running around. Also, Avon Products is experimenting with Warnaco Inc. by including bras and sleepwear under the Warners, Fruit of the Loom, and Scaasi labels through their Avon door-to-door sales force. Wal-Mart, is partnering with Ronald McDonald, in their recently completed Wal-Mart store in Oxnard, California. Proudly displayed, are signs on the store's entrance doors announcing, *McDonald's inside* and a life-size plastic Ronald, sits inside on a bench to greet customers.

• Rather than owning and operating a manufacturing plant, a synergistic partnering agreement allows you to have elements of your product or the entire product built in plants (owned by others or in joint venture) with the most up to date technology. This is the idea behind the Donnelly Corporation and their venture with Applied Films Laboratory, Inc. for manufacturing and supplying the world market in display coated glass for liquid crystal displays (LCDs).

• Just-in-time inventory purchasing and supplying as exemplified by the much talked about relationship between Wal-Mart and Procter & Gamble.

• Greater consistency in parts, supplies, semi-assembled, and completed products, as will be detailed later in Steelcase's supplier certification program.

• "Big benefit of partnering," says Jim Eisenhart, president of Ventura Consulting Group, Inc., Ventura, California, "is it puts pleasure and fun back into [construction] business." People are now open to partnering because they recognize the limits of old paradigms, [adversarial] especially in the context of global competition."[11]

• The Arizona and California Departments of Transportation have so successfully discovered that the partnering approach benefits many industries' experience, especially, the construction industry, by eliminating the tangle of claims, litigation, and adversarial relationships through a concept of cooperation throughout the life of a project. And by identifying potential relationship hazards. Benchmarking, (companies sharing information on what they do best) especially in the aerospace industry, has shown increased productivity and decreased costs across the board.

Additionally, you'll find that partnering can provide the benefit of positioning for future needs not yet known to you or your industry. An example, a lead-user firm is one whose present needs will reflect its segment's needs in future months or years. Through partnering, a company can assist another to leap-frog current industry leaders by cooperating with newer firms more willing to pursue a riskier development strategy to gain market share. This strategy can aid companies, large and small, in more rapidly and efficiently reaching their collective goals.

Productivity increases are also achieved through partnering. "Brown & Root/Braun has been a partner with Union Carbide Corp., Danbury, Conn., for three years. B&R/B studied about 18 projects during that period and concluded that productivity on partnering jobs was about 16% to 17% better than previous levels.[12]

Further partnering benefits include: complementing individual skill sets through cooperative alliances, pooling of resources, economies of scale, financial stability, and bundling of a partner's goods and services. Such as snack manufacturers who are now mixing two nationally known names and logos on a single product. An example of this is Betty Crockers' Soda·Licious, soda pop fruit snacks, made with 7UP and 7UP Cherry. Be sure you understand what it is that you are trying to get out of each of your partnering efforts!

Finally, and decisively important, is that when a company embraces the philosophy of partnering the result will be, through cooperation and collaboration, an increase in quality. As the various areas of the pentad partnership begin to develop, pay particular attention to the pentad as a whole. This will increase the quality and productivity of the interdependent pentad relationships. Total Quality Management, (TQM) is made possible through partnering.

Ultimately the benefit to partnering with others is for solutions—solutions to your problems and those of your customers. It's rare that a company can be all things to all people—yet, through adopting the partnering paradigm, you will get much closer than without.

A NEW BELIEF

Partnering. Just another in the parade of management impulses? An instant panacea to the setbacks and challenges that American business faces today? The answer to both is a resounding no!

In 1496, just a few years after Christopher Columbus set off to discover The New World, and shattering conventional wisdom about the known world being flat, Nicholas Copernicus enrolled in the University of Bologna as a student of canon law. Privately, Copernicus pursued his interest in astronomy, making his earliest recorded observation in 1497. Some time before May 1, 1514, he wrote the first draft of his new astronomical system, *De hypothesibus motuum coelestium a se constitutis commentarious* and discreetly circulated a few manuscript copies among trusted friends—challenging our place in the universe.

In the same spirit, I challenge your business paradigm, your belief of how modern business is to be conducted. Not just challenge you, but give you an alternative business paradigm for success—Partnering.

Copernicus, who faced and received excommunication from his faith for boldly pushing the limits (in 1992, the Pope reversed the order), as do modern day heros, it takes putting your reputation on the line to effectively create change. Are you willing to do the same? "What's it going to take to get you and/or your company to change?

Why a need for a new business belief? To succeed, you must adopt or at least adapt to, new ideas. Your business relationships will mean success or failure as you move into the new millennium. Most of all though, it's time! Time for a paradigm that is realistic to its possibilities, and can assist goal achievement—whether entrepreneurial or corporate.

A most important lesson I learned is that everybody wants to feel good about themselves and will do "what it takes" to get to that place. Partnering, as I have defined it, will do this because an equality of partners is developed, while position, power and prestige are allowed to stay intact. Today there is much talk about empowerment but unfortunately many people of "position power" (authority based in their title) believe their power must diminish at the same rate that power is given to others. This is completely untrue. The giving of power creates more power and this class of power is the most powerful of all—it's "personal power" (ability to influence others because of who you are)! When people want to partner with you...that's personal power. When you want to partner with others, you also increase this personal power.

In a recent *Nation's Business*, Pamela Coker, Founder, President, and CEO of Acucobol, Inc. in San Diego, California stated, "Love your customers, employees, shareholders, vendors, and community—in that order—and the profits will follow." This partnering philosophy has elevated Acucobol, from a start-up company of six people to an international software company with annual sales soaring to over $4 million in 40 months. After the company's initial year of operation, profits began and have continued to flow since.

Another partnering lesson I've learned is getting along with other departments, and working together for the good of the entire company. We will call this internal or interdepartmental partnering. Just think how much better you could partner with your customers and employees if your employees partnered with each other. Internal politics, as I first learned at Yosemite National Park is a fatal flaw that many companies must overcome. Still, as a manager, it was my responsibility to get along with others—I was a resounding failure at it!

All sectors, public and private, are now slowly discovering that it is more cost effective to develop a win-win business relationship than to constantly make expensive changes for a penny or two savings. Sure, everybody wants great prices and unsurpassed service—yet many are finding that to get both, a partnering relationship must be developed…and that doesn't happen over night! This was Sam Walton's (founder of Wal-Mart, nation's largest retailer) paradigm of success. He was the retail sector's embodied proof of the value of partnering. Walton referred to and treated all employees as associates and early in the company's history he saw to it that the associates shared in the profits.

WHAT'S NEEDED TO MAKE PARTNERING WORK

Financial Network Investment Corporation (FNIC) has built their success on the partnering foundation. From the beginning when Miles Gordon, CEO partnered with others to develop the network of independent securities broker/dealers, and to the present, as it is now one of the largest in the United States, the partnering conviction has remained part of the fabric of their culture. Gordon recommends:

"Choose your people carefully. Choosing your people is probably the most important thing. In any of the different lines—it cuts across all the lines. Within our own system, the optimal—if you have a good representative, good manager, good regional director, it works out well. Where you don't, it typically has not worked out well. With a vendor, this is clearly the case. Synergistically, whether it be accountants, lawyers, brokers of other industries, mortgage brokers, real estate brokers, know the people. If you have good people over there they will attract good people."[13]

Steelcase Inc., with headquarters in Grand Rapids, Michigan, is a privately held firm with worldwide sales in 1991 of $2.3 billion and employees totaling over 20,000 (over 12,000 in the U.S.). With 42 manufacturing plants in 11 countries, Steelcase has 20.6 million square feet of manufacturing, shipping and administrative facilities worldwide.

Industry Week claims that [in North America] Steelcase, "...has more than double the market share of its nearest competitor."[14] Founded in 1912, with sales of $13,000—Steelcase North America's sales in 1990 were almost $2 billion. Partnering has been at the core of their corporate culture as long as anybody can remember. In fact, their dealer network is based on a handshake agreement.

Roger Choquette, Vice President of Dealer Alliances at Steelcase is responsible for the departments that provide services to their more than 500 independently owned and operated dealerships (synergistic alliances) in North America, and is the first in his position to hold the title of Vice President. Choquette shared his feelings about partnering:

> "When we specifically talk about Steelcase and you begin to explore the concept of partnering, I think we are basically talking about an alignment toward common goals that ultimately result in success and profitability in the marketplace for both of us. In other words, whatever we do together in the marketplace needs to be done in cognizance of the other party. We need to win together, we need to lose together. We can't go into a situation and try to achieve something without thinking of the impact on the other partner."[15]

Cascade Engineering, Grand Rapids, Michigan is an innovative injection molder of plastics for several industries, including: automotive, furniture, and containers (using a 9,000-ton injection machine). Over the past few years they have learned much about partnering. Dave Barrett, Project Manager at Cascade retold a splendid story about being a plant manager and a group of employees wanted to partner with him to develop a self-directed work team. Barrett has this to say about partnering:

> "There's got to be mutual respect, you can't go in with a baseball bat, you can't go in with the hammer down. You have to go in with the idea that you really want to work with a group of people or an individual— not arm twisting until they conform—but rather very open.
> Have something you're attempting to accomplish—don't just go in and say, 'Hey, I'm here to partner with you.' It's better say, 'Let's sit down, we have this problem and we have a problem solving method that we've previously used to work through that sort of problem.' Of course you can state your expectations, but don't do it in a demanding tone."[16]

Founded in 1956 by <u>Jan</u> and <u>Fran</u>k Day, Jafra Cosmetics International is a subsidiary of The Gillette Company and is based in Westlake Village, California. Their products are sold in 13 countries, including the United States, Europe, Mexico, Central and South America through independent consultants. Worldwide, Jafra has more than 186,000 active, independent consultants, including 60,000 in the United Stated. Pat Krupa, Training Director, Lineage (consultant) Management, says:

> "Everybody wants to feel important. When you understand that, then in any arena that you are dealing with a person, the most important thing is letting that person know that they are important. Important to your company, to the people in your family, that you have value and worth, and that you're appreciated for every effort that you try."
> "I think to a manager's staff in a corporation or to a district director, what she needs to give to her people is belief that they are valuable, belief that they are important, belief that they matter, belief that every single time that they pick up the phone and get a 'NO!' or

rescheduling of their Jafra class, that they still matter.

One of the reasons that people don't succeed is that they feel that it [their job] doesn't matter to anybody. If they sell a product—who is it going to matter to? To the person who receives the product—it makes a difference in self perception. It makes a difference to the person who starts doing Jafra because one of our consultants influenced her to join and it changes her life completely. I am—we are—in the business of changing lives.[17]

Leon R. Slikkers started at Chris-Craft in the jointer department making cabin tops in 1946 and has been making boats ever since. Today, he, along with all four of his offspring are part of the privately held, S2 Yachts, Inc., in Holland, Michigan. They have nearly 6000,000 square feet of plant space at their 80-acre tract in Holland and 20-acre site in Fort Pierce, Florida. They are known for producing some of the highest quality yachts available worldwide.

David Slikkers, eldest son of Leon is President and believes that partnering with his customers and employees can make the difference in producing quality and turning a profit. When asked about partnering with his suppliers; he thinks the suppliers to his industry are about three years behind in understanding his needs. He says this about partnering:

"From a partnering standpoint, I'd want to believe this is someone, the same as I, who has a vested interest in the outcome. In partnering, I have to be willing to take on the responsibility of what a partner means and shoulder the responsibility on whatever project that happens to be. Whether that means a particular task or building something—I'm going to have some responsibility because someone is going to be counting on me. And I in turn, am going to lean on somebody else."[18]

Edward Howard, Director, Market Management, Worldwide Alliance Division at Steelcase states:

"What you're on [partnering] is hopefully the taproot, the main source of how America moves forward. Customers have to be in the partnering process. They have to see that I'm not letting the wolf into the hen house. But, what is Partnering [with customers]? We want the end user when they leave that work environment to say, at the end of the day, 'These really worked well.'"[19]

Mitsubishi Motor Sales of America, Inc., located in Cypress, California commenced selling automobiles in the U.S. in 1982, and sold 5,214 that year. Through a reputation for quality, style, high technology, and affordability, Mitsubishi has grown to selling almost 200,000 cars in 1992. Though Japanese owned, the many Americans working there perceive themselves as an American company. They have gone through some excruciating growing pains in their effort to become a company of vision and based on my research I believe partnering is a large part of that vision. Tom Benson, Vice President Service and Customer Management (retired, Fall 1993) of Mitsubishi shares what he thinks is the key to partnering:

"People pretty much operate based on their values and I think the key to partnering is to somehow align the values—I'm not talking about ethics, but in order for a partnership to work people have to have a common understanding of values. I think maybe in the [automobile] dealerships of today—the values of the dealerships too often aren't in line with the values of their customer. If I could somehow figure out how to align these values, then we could develop a partnership based on that common set of values."[20]

Jim Rutherford, Manager, Marketing Communications at Steelcase, had some strong feelings about partnering. He is the senior member of the team that interacts with Peerless Lighting in Berkeley, California, an alliance partner. Daily, he lives and breaths synergistic alliances, and this is what he had to say:

"To me, partnering, by definition, has to be both customer focused and selfish. There has to be a motivation in partnering to provide both partners' and their mutual customer with added value. But I believe if it does not also provide instrumental profits to both partners because of the synergy of the relationship, that you don't really get the full benefit that you could. You could be altruistic about it and say, 'Well, I'm adding value to my customer and the other partner is taking all the money, but at least I'm getting some of the credit.' If that credit doesn't translate into increased sales, why do it?"[21]

Above, you have met some of the people I interviewed in my research for *The Art of Partnering*, you'll hear more from these dynamic and bold individuals and from others whom I believe, have some insight on partnering.

PARADIGM INTRODUCTION

The introduction of a new paradigm or belief need not be difficult if approached with reason. Prove it to yourself with this simple test: Draw yourself a bath of luke warm water, get in the tub and relax. Next, open the water valve allowing only hot water into the tub. Let the hot water run for as long as you can stand the heat. Use a thermometer to record the water temperature. The next day, draw yourself a bath at that same maximum temperature. Chances are you'll jump out of the tub... the water will be too hot for you. Why was it tolerable before? You became accustom to the change slowly. Eventually, you'll ease into the tub—as it cools and you get acclimated to the heat. Similarly, we humans prefer to ease into change. Too much change, too quick can be fatal! Give yourself and all the people around you time to adjust to the "hot water" or shifting paradigm.

Partnering alliances are available for those who are willing to make available the necessary time commitment, be prepared for, and believe in, the power of partnering. Being prepared is guaranteed to be a difficult endeavor and I assure you that as a result of reading this book you will have an earnest idea of what you can expect.

The time commitment is an absolute necessity in developing relationships, just as in any partnering endeavor...set your partnering plan into play and avoid the urge to change it before the plan has time to work. It's up to you—the belief in partnering. Be ready for ridicule from non-believers—it's sure to come.

Doing business through a partnering window will open up new possibilities for your management, production, and marketing strategy as well as your business as a whole. You will learn how to work with others for cost reductions while enjoying greater than ever exposure to your current market, as well as to other markets. You can succeed and you can do it with others. The basic concept is to make the pie bigger than ever before, and helping others as well as yourself to a bigger piece than previously believed possible. Embrace Integrity Partnering and enjoy the dividends of your effective effort.

Roger Tompkins promotes the idea of overlapping areas of interest to increase partnering success. Tompkins' insights:

- "The more closely the circles of interest overlaps, the more likely the partnership is to succeed."
- "The closer each treats the other as he/she would like to be treated in the same circumstances, the better the partnership works."[22]

DO NOT WAIT FOR PERFECTION

If you wait for things to be perfect, it'll be too late. Your competition will do what you simply thought about. This dilemma has been called *paralysis by analysis*. Get started, get some momentum going and then pause for accuracy or course correction. Did you know that an experienced airline pilot will change course over 400 times in flight from Los Angeles to Hawaii? It's continuous, so don't get discouraged if you get a little off-course once in a while.

I'll share with you Dr. Terry Paulson's Three P's: Perfection, which leads to Procrastination, which leads to Paralysis.[23] Don't become paralysed; you can't make any money that way. As hockey star, Wayne Gretzky says, "You miss 100% of the shots you never take."

Lee Iacocca says that 95% is good enough, if you wait for the last 5% to be just right, what you were working on becomes obsolete.[24] Quality remains the goal by the time it reaches the customer, but getting started allows you to experience mistakes early, before they cost you.

Studying a challenge is usually considered to be a strength. What happens when you study infinitum? Your perceived strength can also become a weakness. The result is what I just mentioned, lack of action, and there's one more consideration...being perceived by your partners, peers, and/or superiors as not having the ability to make a decision. This can be all too costly in your business or career. The ability to make decisive and timely decisions is at the root of leadership. Being perceived by your industry as a waffler can be the kiss of death. You will be excluded from new and exciting partnering alliances because others will not think you can be depended upon.

Risk taking is also crucial to partnering, and yet taking imprudent, irresponsible, and reckless risks puts the core foundation, so important to building relationships, in jeopardy. Early in my career, an executive would repeatedly say this to me about risk taking, "Ed, if you're not making mistakes; I don't need you because you're not taking risks and learning. But, if you keep making the same mistakes I don't need you either, because you're not learning." One of the great values you'll receive from partnering is access to the mistakes of others—reducing the need to take uninformed risks.

I'm not suggesting you eliminate risk taking—I'm simply suggesting you be smart in application. By eliminating needless risk, you will profit from both the success and failures of your partners.

PARTNERING PITFALLS—CAVEAT PARS

Partnering, as with anything else has pitfalls and unexpected land mines. Business consultant and author of *76 Ways to Build a Straight Referral Business—ASAP!*, Lorna Riley, suggests that conflict, which can be a tragic pitfall, emanates from four core areas: values, goals, facts, and procedures. Conflict doesn't have to be a road block to partnering if you and your partnering alliance members are willing to resolve the conflict at the core level, in a timely manner. In fact, the resolved conflict can lead to a stronger relationship through improved communication. Unfortunately, conflict that is left unresolved will lead to fatal flaws that will erode the relationship.

To date, the alliance mortality rate is fifty percent.[25] If you wait to build partnering relationships until all the potential pitfalls are unearthed, your industry will pass you by—those you might have considered as possible members for partnering alliances, will be partnering with your competition. Be realistic though, as with a spouse, partnering alliance members don't change with time to become, who and what you want them to be, but rather, evolve to who and what they desire. If you suspect core problems, you probably are accurate in your assessment and the chances for a successful alliance is greatly diminished. *Partnering, like a marriage, will not change people.*

Founded in 1905, Donnelly Corporation in Holland, Michigan started as a glass mirror manufacturer and supplier for the turn-of-the-century furniture industry. With net sales in 1993 of over $300 million, along with other endeavors, and supplying rear view mirrors to automobile manufacturers in the approximate amounts of: 90% in North America, 50% in Japan, and 50% in Europe they are successfully partnering around the globe, having developed four joint ventures and seven strategic alliances.

Dwane Baumgardner, Ph.D., Chairman & CEO at Donnelly feels strongly about what it takes to be successful at partnering. He told me, "If you have management that is not operating on the basic believe—that it has to start at the top—those beliefs have to be held and permeated throughout the organization [for partnering to work]. For example, with employees, if you don't believe your people can be trusted, that they want to work together in a supportive and cooperative fashion—same with another company—you have to believe when you form a strategic alliance with another company, that they will operate with the same motive that you operate and that they want you to be successful just like they want to be successful, so you can trust them. If you don't have those beliefs, I think you're going to run into problems."[26]

Trust in others and the belief that partnering starts at the top, are topics that will frequently be covered in the pages to come. I see these two topics as core causes for failed partnering agreements when they're not followed. Also, be cautious of things you can't see now but may experience later—like the small print on page 37, clause 5, paragraph 2, of a 70 page contract. Don't let your rose colored lens jade your judgement. Caveat emptor, buyer beware, should be changed to caveat pars, partner beware, just because you're working with a company of integrity—it doesn't mean they will look out for you. Even in a partnering relationship, you are still accountable for your own well being.

Are you simply looking for more sales volume and profits? Make sure your bottom-line expectations take into account that servicing the partnering agreement is likely to require more resources. DuPont Construction Manager, Jack R. Farmer, Jr. believes, "If the contractor is looking just to maximize his profits on just one job, then partnering is not for him."[27] Be sure of everybody's partnering goals. Here are a few examples of potential pitfalls, study them before you enter an agreement and your chances for success will profusely increase:

•   Underestimating the complexity of coordinating and integrating corporate resources, and overestimating your partner's abilities to achieve the end result. Eventually, partnering success depends on the managers' abilities, skills, aspirations and passions to assemble the pieces of the puzzle.

• Situations where a customer is the driving force behind a partnering arrangement, be sure to examine each proposal in the context of your company's overall partnering strategy.

• Not having access to a partners employees. The closer the planned relationship between the two companies, the greater the importance of the linkages between them.

• A large company partners with a small; the representatives, usually top executives, of the small can make decisions on the spot but the employees of the giant must take a proposal up the chain of command. This policy can become frustrating for the small.

• One partner not completely embracing the principles of partnering at the top level or even in departments, divisions or regions while the other does. BE&K has been involved in a partnering relationship with DuPont since 1986. BE&K, President, T. Michael Goodrich states, "If the commitment is not there from the top to the bottom of the organization, the partnering concept will not work."[28]

• Partners have different core values—like trust and integrity or there are corporate culture clashes, employee turf protection, and resistance of some employees to new ideas, these issues can reek havoc.

• Partners internal reward structure. In partnering with customers or suppliers—traditional reward for buyers comes with wringing out concessions from the seller and by showing that their efforts had achieved cost reductions. On the flip side, sellers usually reward for sales performance.

• Third party not playing ball, (ie., physicians with employer-provider partnerships not going along with program). All the elemental members of a partnering agreement will have to "give a little" for the agreement to work. Also, a partners' unexpected inefficiencies or poor management practices can be the demise of a well-intended partnering plan.

• If a partner receives unfavorable media coverage you are pulled into the picture. Real or perceived, image and reputation are critical to a company's success.

•   When sitting down at the partnering table a partner might find the partnering seat uncomfortable. It could be that your partner has a different level of emotional and physical comfort, or sometimes it is simply a change in corporate strategy or a restructuring which leads away from a partner's product and/or technology causing the partners distress.

•   After making a partnering commitment, a partner may have a hidden agenda or decide they don't like or want to follow through with that which they committed, or does not have the capability to do what is necessary.

•   Contracts with an overseas market, for instance, often take a long time to finalize. By the time you get going, in the technology industries, your competition may have already started.

•   Difficulty communicating across various time zones. Solving problems quickly when your partnering factory is located halfway around the world is hard enough when you speak the same language. Add the increased difficulty of language barriers, and major challenges can emanate from the alliance.

•   The disloyalty that can occur when you try to partner with a potential or current customer and have them renege on the promise of purchasing from you after you have delivered complementary or introductory training. Adding insult to injury, they go to one of your competitors seeking only a better price. There is also the possibility of one unethical partner attempting to capture another's technology or trade secrets. Use caution when offering education or assistance.

•   When unequal dependence in a relationship occurs, the partner with the least dependence could be less likely to compromise and expend energy into the relationship.

•   Complacency, is an insidious relationship-killer. Continuously ask questions in a way that encourages partners to relate problems and shortcomings. Ask, "What have we *not* done lately?"

•   Meanings assigned to words by different cultures can cause serious problems. This was the case in the alliance Steelcase has with Peerless Lighting. Steelcase dealers were told that Peerless was *responsive*, and in the Steelcase culture, responsive means overnight delivery for trade show materials. When dealers would contact Peerless with a similar request, they were told it wouldn't be possible because of production time. "The thing is, when we said they're [Peerless] responsive, they were, but we never bothered to define what that means," states Jim Rutherford at Steelcase.[29]

•   Unrealistic expectations of any partner's capabilities—these areas include: technology, research, production skills, marketing might, and financial backing.

Now that you've had a view of partnering from the down-side, don't let these hurdles stop you. Having knowledge of the "partnering unknown" should keep you from becoming immobilized and waiting for opportunities that could easily pass you by. Sure, there are some risks, but to lessen the effects, David Elliott, Senior Vice President and Chief Administrative Officer at Technicolor, Inc. in North Hollywood, California shares his thoughts.

> "If a partner fails to meet their responsibilities, a clear agenda is necessary that both sides are operating from. When the agendas are different or conflicted—it's a problem. We don't have partnering horror stories because we include an exit strategy, before going into the relationship. You're to set milestones going into the agreement. In order for us to continue—be it a vendor or service support relationship, these milestones are necessary. If they're not met we make some changes."[30]

Elliott's advice for others entering into partnering relationships is to do your homework, know the agenda of all partners in the relationship and measure against it. If after doing your homework you're still not completely sold on partnering with a company, start small. Begin your alliance by partnering with another for a simple or small promotion and get your feet wet. If you do stumble—having the ability to regenerate after a fall is crucial, especially if you or a partner simply make a mistake. When events and circumstances are not what you had hoped or planned for—be careful—you might go to a place of apathy. If you remain in a toxic mind-set, you'll wait and wait for things to get better before you move into action. The trouble is that things rarely get better until you propel yourself into a state of activity.

To be successful at partnering you must commit to functioning at a higher level—one that will allow you to stretch your comfort zone and then commit to moving into action. Without these two issues in concert, you might not get started or re-started when necessary.

Once you get back in the action, you can go after small wins to reestablish your confidence to take risks in pursuit of an even larger prize. The key is to not wait for all to be perfect before you commence. It's okay to "ready, shoot, aim," in fact, I prefer it. Do though, take the time to adjust your aim after you begin—be like the pilot and course correct regularly. Keep your future focus on the partnering journey. Keep it improving—be decisive, and show the qualities of a leader in your industry. You will be rewarded.

TWO

INITIATING THE PARTNERING PROCESS

In his paper, *Commentariolus*, Copernicus, the founder of modern astronomy, disputed the astronomical system which had overshadowed Western thought since the days of Aristotle and Ptolemy. Copernicus heralded that "the center of the earth is not the center of the universe." Apply this to partnering and my stand is: The company and its owner/executives, are not at the center and are not the most important element in today's global economy.

You may argue that, "Without me and/or my company, there's no need for employees, suppliers, and customers." "We revolve about the sun like any other planet," said Copernicus, assigning the earth to its rightful place in the cosmos. Today, business is global or globally effected. The business playing field has changed, you would be less than successful attempting to play soccer on a baseball diamond.

Copernicus was not the first to assert the motion of the earth. Two Pythagoreans, Philolaus and Ecphantus, were credited by Copernicus as being the genesis of his work. Similarly, I'm not the first to suggest partnering. By identifying the five primary areas for business relationships, I am recommending that you too, can discover the connection each has to the other, and develop your partnering pentad. In the rest of this book, I will demonstrate the elements necessary to build your own pentad using the star graphic at the top of the page as a model in consideration of the Copernican universe.

DEVELOP YOUR PARTNERING PENTAD

The Copernican Pentad consists of the following members: **synergistic alliances, suppliers, customers, employees,** and **the executive/the company.** Focusing on the five areas, I'll share insights for developing these, as well as examples of people and businesses who have successfully developed one or more partnering elements of the pentad within their business. Ultimately, you want to concentrate not on one at a time, but concurrently on all the areas. Growing in one area at the cost of the other areas will not serve your efforts.

A business, like the human body has many parts: The brain might equate to the executive suite, the hands could parallel manufacturing, and a good argument could be given as to why the feet are similar to sales and marketing. The other organs and body parts could also be equated to business functions. Finger nails might represent over grown deadwood employees and equipment which must be clipped. The collective body parts and organs are necessary parts of the whole. As you know, your body does not operate as efficiently as possible without all the pieces.

The partnering pentad idea functions under the same belief—that a company and all of its parts must perform their functions keeping in mind how independent actions affect the other parts. For years, interdepartmental cooperation has been merely an idea and nothing more, similar to cotton candy partnering. Think of it as eating something you are allergic to just to satisfy a need—it's the same principal when one department knowingly does something that will have an adverse consequence to another department.

Integrity partnering is as much the answer to successful internal cooperation as it is to external alliances. No company can succeed if its inner workings are being ripped apart at the seams by distrust, individual protectionism, and poor communications. Examples of this destruction are all too easy to find—possibly as easy as looking at your own company.

> "Something you have to pay close attention to, like setting up a strategic alliance with another company, you can't just negotiate an agreement with someone at my level and then just walk away and say, 'Well, gee, we have our alliance in place.'" Dwane Baumgardner at Donnelly continues, "It requires constant attention to make it work—any kind of relationship. Same things with employees. It requires hard work a continued struggle. That's part of working together and trying to improve, however it doesn't always go smooth. Also, with other companies, one of the things we always do is have a specific individual that we identify with internally. We constantly think about and maintain contact with this person."[31]

Internal and external cooperation is necessary for successful adaptation of partnering principles. Though many large and rigid companies are looking at partnering possibilities, integrated companies like SMTEK of Newbury Park, California, enjoy higher productivity and lower production costs than many of their giant competitor/customers like Hughes Aircraft, Litton Industries, and Martin Marietta. Integration is accomplished through the interdependence of all departments rather than dependence or independence. Greg Horton, founder and CEO of SMTEK uses the term, "competitor/customer" because, many times he competes with his customer's engineering departments for design contracts (where the profit is). Horton's state-of-the-art robotics production line can produce surface mount technology electronic modules more cost effectively than many of his gigantic customers. Obtaining production contracts enables him access to key design contract decision makers.

Developing products and services, along with marketing efforts is hard enough without having unneeded hurdles to overcome. Partnering is not only an activity but also a mind-set. Partnering is a place where marketing, management, and philosophy meet. Integrated companies also include the marketing department in all aspects of product development and manufacturer. The reason for this is that you can be the best at developing and cost effectively producing a product that absolutely nobody wants. As with bringing in the marketing department from a product's conception for the purpose of making it more marketable, this book will show you how to partner as a whole and complete business—while staying aware of the specific needs of the relationships in your partnering pentad.

PARTNERING CORE VALUES

To start, you must adopt the core values to successful relationships which are basically synonymous with those of partnering:

Trust. Trust, as mentioned earlier by Dwane Baumgardner, is defined as confidence; a reliance or resting of the mind on the integrity, veracity, justice, friendship, or other sound principle of another person or thing. It's also the glue that binds an organization together. For partnering, trust is necessary to move from inertia to action. Trust is that wonderful, mystical and cherished virtue hoped for and shared among practitioners of the Partnering Paradigm.

In trust, you're continually putting yourself at risk. It's the process of taking risks necessary in building relationships. At times you are certain to be disappointed, but hopefully these disappointments will be few, compared to the availability of beneficial experiences.

Tolerance/Understanding. It's unfortunate, that the words tolerance and understanding, have become a cliche that too easily rolls off the tongue. For partnering to work, this core value must be *cherished and practiced* by all in the alliance. When you can accept the value of an idea rather than be concerned by who's inspiration it was conceived, you will truly exhibit tolerance and understanding.

Cooperation/Growth. In my seminars, I lead exercises like one where the audience is standing in a circle and facing to the center, blindfolded, and holding a rope, they are then instructed to make a square. This exercise and others, were created to show how much more is possible when the participants work together rather than separately. This is only possible when they adopt an attitude of cooperation. During the rope exercise, it is always interesting who shows up as the leader to make the square—it's not always the boss. Growth is the natural outcropping of this essential element.

Caring/Commitment. Caring enough about a partnering alliance and its members to make a commitment to it's success is what will usually smooth out the potholes on the road to successful partnering. It's this element that allows each partner in the alliance to feel they will be heard and remain reasonably safe from criticism. Additionally, there is also the commitment that is necessary to the function of leadership, and at times, the ability to follow when another is currently leading.

Synergy/Mutuality. Partnering must be an institution where individuals, organizations, and companies come together to develop a relationship of trust, tolerance, understanding, cooperation, growth, caring, and commitment. The result being synergy and mutuality—similar to a successful marriage. Partnering and partnerships have much in common with the institution of marriage—both require all of the above, and both offer benefits that out-distance the possibilities available singularly.

When two people enter into marriage the first synergistic result is one plus one equaling three: she, he, and they. The "they" takes on a new life while the "she' and "he" retain their unique individuality. This is the successful formula both for marriage and partnering.

The preceding values were prevalent in every successful partnering alliance I have studied. In a symbiotic relationship, that of two dissimilar organisms in close association or union, especially where this is advantageous to both, each finds a way to co-exist. The partner or partners you select must also adopt these core values or the relationship is doomed to failure from its inception, never allowing symbiosis to occur.

Couple the above with "the desire to win" and you now have the foundation for successful partnering alliances. These alliances form the framework for a marketing campaign and business strategy based on partnering. The reason I suggest this is because partnering alliances are only as strong as their weakest member. When the weakest member does not have the desire to win, they become nothing more than a remora—a fish that adheres to another that can only be dislodged with difficulty—hanging on and benefiting from your efforts and contributing nothing! Synergy is a "must have" ingredient in a successful partnering alliance.

State Farm Insurance's Roger Tompkins, shares his three universal principles of partnering, be it partnering at work, school, in the community, or with the family through the following questions:

- "Where does your circle of interest and mine overlap?"
- "How can I help you be successful so that, in turn, you can and will help me?"
- "How can I advance your deepest held interests in such a way that you will help me advance mine?"[32]

Roger Choquette of Steelcase suggests partnering is rooted in four core elements: Mutality, Commitment, Understanding, and Growth—though I believe trust is also a core element and must come first—Roger's valuable thoughts on the subject are:

"Let me just give you a couple of excerpts here. For a partnership to work you have to understand the four elements. The first one is mutuality. Our goals must be mutually agreed upon. I can't bring you my goals and put them on you as your goals. We have to agree what we're going to do together. Our daily tasks must not be mutually exclusive.

Whenever we make a decision we have to think about the impact on the dealer? It takes a long time to develop that, and you have to go through a lot of experience. That means that as a distributor when you represent my product I trust you to think about what you do, day in and day out, not only at the executive level but at the sales rep level. To think about us, you represent my product and representing my product over someone else's product.

Understand this, our dealerships will sell somewhere between 60% and 80% of their gross sales dollars in Steelcase products. We give more than we take. It isn't a compromise situation where I give 50% and you give 50%. You always try to give to the relationship more than you take from it.

We're talking about a partnership here, and it's a two-way partnership. If I give more than I take and you give more than you take, nobody ends up taking advantage of the other person. This isn't our credo, this is a partnership, so I speak for both parties there. Just like our goals. They can't be mutually exclusive.

If you want to make more money, and you represent 60-80% of your gross sales dollar as my product, then we've got to have a conversation at the beginning of the year and you say, 'Roger, I cannot afford to continue to grow my business based on the margins that I currently have. I've got to make this and this investment'. Those are things that I think you're asking me to do. And those are things that I think you're asking me to do. Yes, I am. You've got to help me increase my gross sales dollar.

So together we've got to sit down and figure out how that happens. It isn't a matter of I just give you more money and your dollars go up. Maybe I do in certain situations, decrease my wholesale price. Maybe I help you decrease your expenses. Maybe I help you increase automation so that you can streamline efficiency and so on and so forth. So, if we agree on the mutual goals and then we agree on how to get there, we're going to get there together.

That's how we work with our dealers, so it's not a matter of I come in and I pound you for more sales. I may come in and say, 'hey look, we've got to get 5% more out of this market than we did last year. You're our only dealer in the market so if we don't do it with you we basically don't do it with anybody. How do we get 5% more?' And together we'll sit down with the dealer and he may say, 'here are the things that I think will have to happen. Well, here are some of the things that we think need to happen. Are we connected or disconnected?' Then we sort through it and that becomes the basis for the sales and marketing plan for the following year."[33]

STEPS TO PARTNERING

Step 1: Monitor.

Study your business, observe, and identify areas for improvement. Also, take inventory of core strengths that might be valuable to a potential alliance partner. Specifically, define what it is that you want and help others to define what they want and help them to achieve it as quickly as possible. Study other industries that have embraced partnering along with the individual companies that have been successful with partnering. Study what worked and what did not. If partnering was not successful, be sure to understand why.

Step 2: Educate.

Learn about those companies you might consider for partnering arrangements; Arrangements that create a win-win result for all who participate. Ask yourself and your management team these questions: What are their strengths and weaknesses? What affect would they have on our business and our's on their business? Be sure that the company cultures are complementary and that the people who will make the alliance work have the ability to get along.

Step 3: Select.

This is the critical step—all your future efforts will be built on this foundation. Select partnering, and with whom to partner, with knowledge, understanding and commitment. Surely, there is little security built upon a foundation of fatal flaws. Search for the strongest material for your partnering foundation. Customer-oriented culture is critical to the success of the partnering alliance. The greater the sophistication of a company and its officers, the more likely a company will enter into partnering—keep this in mind when making your selection. Embrace long-term thinking. Partnering is rarely a quick fix, but rather a sound long-term business strategy. Target companies, large or small, that can aid you in rapidly and efficiently, reaching the goals of research, technology, production and marketing.

Another element to consider is the focus of the individuals involved. Be certain their focus of the partnering relationship is strategic to the individuals' goals. A disparity of focus could be unhealthy and put your future alliance at risk.

Step 4: Organize.

Now you're to the point of identifying, understanding, and putting together the possibilities for an alliance. Working with internal and external personnel, developing not only your partnering structure, but also your road map—plan it well. The success of the blending of cultures is pivotal to the success of any partnering alliance, take great pains to insure this achievement. Access is crucial—emphasize the importance of understanding and access to each alliance members' staff. Create a convenient communication system for all partners, especially decision makers. Plan procedures to keep relationships between key people of partnering companies open and constantly alive.

Make sure that all levels of both organizations share the partnering attitude. Stress strong information systems and share information constantly. Such as; electronic data interchange for document savings, inventory control, materials ordering, production, and advertising. Agree on net pricing with your partners and delete "income accounts" (accounting practices) that have nothing to do with your business or the real price of your goods and services—things that only make a singular department look successful.

Look into the future, plan for the long term relationship and encourage strategies that will sustain the relationship through to its conclusion. Phasing in the partnering relationship could be a preferred strategy, as this method will allow partners to have a "get acquainted" time. This can assist in the identification of reaching milestones, successfully or identify the need to reassess before moving on to a higher level in the relationship.

Step 5: Charter.

This is the agreement, whether it be a hand shake or actual contract. Even so, I strongly urge all partnering alliances to put their agreements on paper—it's so much more clear six months or two years later. Each alliance member's commitment to the other, is on paper, and it will smooth a path through the potholes of partnering. Also, your charter should spell out conflict resolution—sure as Murphy's Law, conflict will emerge. Be ready for it and the conflict will be resolved timely and amiably. Have an agreed-upon set of procedures in place that will help resolve the issues that arise. Inevitably, there will be a need for a mechanism to handle things like price increase discussions, inability to ship and dispute resolutions.

Develop a clear agreement on what your goals are and make sure they are measurable. Have a formal mechanism for alliance members to identify the goals, milestones, and turning points crucial to the success of the relationship. Devise some form of evaluation that will measure how well plans have implemented Total Quality Management (TQM) principles. Given that each party views the partnering agreement as a business opportunity, the partnering agreement should establish the terms and conditions under which the partners will resolve questions of frustrated business opportunity. Additionally, consider having the partnering agreement include forms of dispute resolution for more formal arrangements, along with exit strategies as partnering safety valves.

Step 6: Post Agreement.

Regularly review your partnering efforts. Periodically sit down with alliance partners and evaluate whether the relationship should be upgraded, maintained, or downgraded. To continuously improve your business and the quality of the partnering agreement, share information regularly with partners. Discuss opportunities for improvement and ways to enhance performance. At Cascade Engineering, Grand Rapids, Michigan, I was told how the auto manufacturers partnered with them by sending a team to assist in solving a production problem. Favorable public image and stature of all partnering alliance members is necessary to keep the alliance valuable to all. Caveat pars! (Partners beware). You are responsible to select and maintain the alliance you entered. If at the onset it seems too good to be true—it likely is!

Inherent in the process, partnering has benefits and pitfalls. I asked Dwane Baumgardner what they at Donnelly do to keep flare-ups from getting to the point where a relationship must be severed. He said, "Meet with the right people as soon as possible, no matter what level, making sure that all the right people are involved, and talk through the problem. You'll find if you get all the right people there to talk through a problem, almost 100% of the time you're able to work it out."[34]

The benefits usually outweigh the downside if you're careful and methodical in the search for a partner, and in the elements of the arrangement. The road to a successful partnership is filled with obstructions that create fatal flaws in your strategies. Knowing the steps to partnering and how to select the right partner (person, company or association), which has the ability to successfully adopt the partnering paradigm philosophy is the first challenge of partnering.

QUALITIES TO IDENTIFY IN AN ALLIANCE PARTNER

Wants to win. No reason to partner with a loser. The relationship will only bring you, your association or company down to an unacceptable level. You must have a desire to win, to want to do better, to be useful in creating synergy with your partner.

Knows he/she is ultimately responsible for their own success. A person who will partner because he/she understands the value of synergy, knowing when partnering is, and is not, the best choice for the situation. Caveat Pars (Beware of Partner)! Accountability goes both ways, don't always assume that your partner is looking out for your best interest. You are human—and as such, are susceptible to not always acting in *your* partner's best interest.

Is an active listener. To truly keep in touch with the heartbeat of an alliance, active listening is a critical skill. This helps you to know what you need to do and when the other side is falling behind in their commitment to you. Alertness from both sides equals mutual success.

Understands and cares about what drives his/her partners' businesses. Because successful partnering is about synergy, you must consistently give added-value to the relationship (regular relationship bank deposits). The only way to add value is to know what it is that your partner considers valuable in connection to their business.

Responds well to, and acts on feedback. "If you can't take the heat, get out of the kitchen!" The only possibility for a forward and beneficial movement is when leaders are willing to accept council. Not one of us is smart enough to know it all! If this were so, there wouldn't be a need for partnering. Notice I didn't mention criticism—it was intentional!

Is flexible, especially when events or circumstances are not what was expected. If you don't have the ability to change direction when the road ahead is washed out, you'll most likely find yourself wishing for rescuers as you uncontrollably float down the stream. Flexibility is absolutely necessary because things will never be exactly as we expect.

Is trustworthy and has integrity—respects all with whom he/she comes in contact. During my research, I interviewed employees at Steelcase, Inc. in Grand Rapids, Michigan and found this to be the common thread weaving through all the employees from the factory floor to the executive suite.

Seeks win-win arrangements and solutions. Earlier, I stated that you must look after yourself, but if that's all you do, you're of little value as a partner. You must win for the sake of your association or business and at the same time, your partner must also win to motivate a desire for them to continue in the relationship. The partnering advantage becomes stronger the longer the relationship lasts.

Understands that partnering is a relationship of interdependence. Notice I didn't say dependence or independence? Visualize your partner and yourself as partially overlapping circles. The parts that overlap are your area of mutual value. The greater the overlap, the greater the value. This overlapping area is also your area of interdependence. Working together for mutual improvement is one of the great benefits received from partnering.

CREDENTIALS OF YOUR FUTURE PARTNER

Critical elements to consider in selecting a partnering alliance member are their credentials—including the feedback their customers and employees have to offer. This is an important area for you to do your detective work. Discovery of an unacceptable component or enterprise of another's company structure could be the determining factor of the viability of an alliance.

An example might be a company you're partnering with to distribute your products. What you produce might be highly technical and users will need a great amount of set-up assistance. The problem is that your partner's sales manager treats people poorly, causing a frequent turn over of sales representatives. The new representatives try, but are not trained quick enough to serve their (your) customers and your stature in the industry is diminished in the process.

Suppose you were partnering, or even associated with Charles

Keeting or Michael Milken in the late 1980s. Simply, your association with them would have a reverberating influence on the future success of your company. When entering upon a partnering alliance look closely at the credentials of your intended partner which are outlined below:

• Have something new to bring to the party. If you're selling hamburgers, then lettuce, pickles, and catsup are necessary but not innovative. Partnering with someone who only has these to offer is fine, but limiting. Suppose someone could supply you with all of the above, and had guacamole. The guacamole is different, thereby allowing you to create a new product—the guacamoleburger. A partner that had a an innovative method to produce fat-free fried chicken, would also be bringing something new to the party, allowing you to increase your penetration within a limited local market.

• The ability to do and produce what your partner perceives you can (individual or company) through skills, technology and relationships. Partnering agreements are of little value when a partner cannot deliver what is promised. If I have hotdog buns and my partner cannot deliver the promised frankfurters, who needs that partner!

• Having the financial ability to go the course. A failed partner usually leads to a failed alliance.

• Possessing the ability to visualize the possibilities through partnering. Going with the flow can breed a mood of, we vs. them. Company norms and procedures that conflict with the goals of the alliance need to be adjusted, but this can only be accomplished through the strength of corporate vision.

• Cultural compatibility, operates from integrity and is willing to challenge existing personal and corporate paradigms.

• Complimentary core strengths, allowing for benchmarking of overlapping capabilities and the elimination of "recreating of the wheel syndrome."

• The ability to think not only strategically, but also tactically.

The ability to have an overall plan is crucial to any partnering alliance, as is the ability to carry-out that plan through maneuvering and cleverness in developing win-win methods for partnering to work.

THE HOUSE OF PARTNERING

The most comprehensive facility, dedicated to the research and development of new products in the office furniture industry is Steelcase's Corporate Development Center (CDC) opened in May 1989. The $111 million building was designed to provide a creative environment for designers, engineers, and marketers, along with, others involved in collaborative partnering in the product development process. Surrounded by 80 acres of restored North American prairie, the seven-story, 575,000 square-foot, pyramid-shaped building is in the Gaines Township of Suburban Grand Rapids, Michigan.

The restored prairie represents Steelcase's partnering with the community, providing a connection with the past, and the building representing the realizing of the future. Additionally, there was a substantial cost savings. Conventional manicured landscape cannot survive without watering and annual maintenance costs which can equal 75% to 100% of the original installation cost ($800 to $1,200 per acre). In contrast, the prairie only requires a controlled burn in the spring for the first few years and then once every four to five years thereafter at a single burn cost of approximately $1,500 for the entire 80 acres.

Walking through this futuristic work environment, I noticed big open spaces and commons. My guide, Peter Jeff, explained that the building was designed to enhance teamwork—that people work in "neighborhoods" rather than having the engineering department on one floor and marketing on another. Neighborhoods are devoted to a specific product team and are populated by different specialists who are part of that team. Jeff explained that it didn't matter whether an employee was a designer or a tooling engineer, they all worked together.

I marveled at what was available to those, fortunate enough, to work there or even lucky enough to visit. For nearly three years, organizational psychologists at three major universities Thomas J. Allen, Ph.D. from MIT, Frank Becker, Ph.D. from Cornell, and Fritz Steele, Ph.D. from Yale acted as consultants with Steelcase in developing the CDC. The objective in erecting this edifice, was to design a creative environment that fostered increased interaction—spontaneous and planned—among designers, engineers, and others involved in the product development process.

Ed Howard, Director, Corporate Marketing for Worldwide Alliance has his office in this building. In asking him about the CDC building, he responded:

"On the job training can occur almost within an hour's notice here. You can get the right people together with the right tools to train others so that the team can move forward. This is a microcosm of Steelcase.

You can start on the lower level which in fact, is a furniture manufacturer, we can literally produce products in the lower level. The upper levels are the research centers. We can go all the way from concept of a new article that comes in from wherever to the resource center on top. You can network with the marketing people, with the product engineering people, the manufacturing engineering people, the design, the fabric selection people, the material management people, all of those entities reside here in some capacity, and you can get through the concept, even a prototype of the product extremely efficiently, and very quickly.

Within a few months, you can have a first production or a pilot run of the product built right here in this building and you can look at it. The team can say, 'oh, I didn't think it was going to look like that' or have other valuable conversations.

This industry is so image oriented and with greater computer graphics capabilities—for the more image conscious, we have the ability to prototype materials very quickly right here in the building. This cuts down thousands of man hours in terms of convincing people where we're going. We can say and show—is this really the idea that you think the customer is looking for?

We have scheduled collaborative and engineering meetings here in the building where their teams come in and look at concepts, they can take shots at them, they can compliment them, they can redirect them, and that's what we feed on, that customer input."[35]

The CDC, to Steelcase represents a new era, a new culture of cooperation, and a desire to understand others' views and needs—a monument to the partnering paradigm. Though you may not desire or find it fiscally possible to erect an edifice, symbols of your commitment to partnering will cement your efforts as a reminder to all that your paradigm in partnering is grounded in integrity rather than cotton candy.

THREE

SYNERGISTIC ALLIANCES

Every successful partnering practitioner learns when it's advantageous, to be and not to be, part of an alliance. Chrysler partners with Mitsubishi, IBM with Apple, and Nestle with Coke—when and where it's in their interest. In each case, the companies formed strategic joint partnerships and alliances that created synergy in their research, manufacturing and marketing. Synergy, simply put, is when the sum of the alliance equals more than the sum of its separate parts ($1 + 1 = 3$).

Disneyland has an official airline, car rental company, and even a cruise ship line. The companies who partner with Disney get more than just marketing exposure; they get positioning and credibility.

What can you do to create synergistic alliances that help you? For example you own a travel agency. Visit all the businesses you can and offer them your extra travel posters and maybe even a trip that you received at no charge, for their promotions. Let them know what you want in exchange. How about the opportunity to post your business name, address, and phone number in a noticeable location for all their customers to see. Maybe they could name you in their newspaper, television and/or radio advertising?

Ask yourself, "Who can I partner with that's not a competitor?" or "Can I partner with a competitor?" How can I be a partner in this relationship? Be sure to make it a synergistic and long term partnership. It's easier to keep a quality relationship going than to develop new ones.

CRITERIA FOR SYNERGISTIC ALLIANCES

David Elliott, Senior Vice President and Chief Administrative Officer at Technicolor, Inc., believes that there is criteria necessary for an alliance:

- Forward thinking.
- A risk taking environment.
- Customer focus.
- A culture of change, creativity, and customer service.

In keeping a business on track and successful, he stated, "We want to change the culture without disrupting our fundamental core business that's been here for a very long time and is very successful."[36] In developing alliances, make certain to use caution when starting to "adjust" your business mix, making a cognizant decision about how the transformation will affect your core business.

TYPES OF SYNERGISTIC ALLIANCES

Synergistic alliances can be broken down into subcategories based on the goal or purpose for the alliances. The following are the general categories I've identified:

Synergistic Alliances for research. The big three U.S. auto makers and the federal government have taken a lesson and created a collaborative effort adapted from Japan's elaborate ties between government and key industries. The consortia have been working on electric-car technology. During a first-ever gathering of more than 200 federal scientists from 12 leading national research laboratories with GM's own engineers and scientists, they said that they expect to deny foreign auto makers access to the fruits of their joint research.[37]

An Environmental Protection Agency (EPA)/Amoco (oil company) test finds that costly rules focus on the wrong part of plants. The study known as the Yorktown Project employed an alliance between unlikely partners. It started out as a chance meeting of old acquaintances aboard a Chicago-to-Washington flight. One, an EPA employee and the other an Amoco employee. It was plenty of work, and came close to doom but the relationship prevailed. The result was that the EPA had a hands-on opportunity to research, and found that many of their assumptions were incorrect.[38]

Synergistic Alliances for Product Development. Chrysler and Westinghouse collaborated to develop a practical electric vehicle. Their 1992 multimillion-dollar joint project was intended to develop an advanced electric motor and power controller, that would boost acceleration and operating range between charges in Chrysler electric vehicles—two previous key limitations.[39]

Kaleida Labs, an Apple-IBM joint venture, is searching for ways to develop multimedia technologies. Their charge: "Kaleida software will form the basic standard for a new genre of devices that read text and images from special compact disks, communicate with new interactive television networks and generally render a rich variety of electronic information accessible to the average consumer."[40]

Synergistic Alliances for Manufacturing and Construction. The construction industry has been forced to partner because of the litigation explosion over the past couple decades. What the industry currently calls "partnering," is for all the key people involved on a project to attend a workshop. There are four basic components to a construction project: The owner, the general contractor, architectural and engineering, and the sub-contractors—all are required to attend this one to five day workshop to air their grievances on each other and iron out their differences. Doing this allows them to write a partnering charter, which all in attendance signs. Basically, they agree to complete the project on time, within budget and without litigation. The idea started at the Army Corps of Engineers and has spread to other government and private sectors.

The Arizona Department of Transportation has made partnering an integral part of their process. For example, a $52 million bid project yielded an average time saved of 19.45%, a savings of $418,203 for Arizona DOT, and a total project savings for all involved of $2,329,026.[41] This is just one example of the many projects where "Partnering" has saved both time and money.

"Partnering offers a new paradigm for owner/contractor relationships," Charles E. Cowan, Director of Arizona Department of Economic Security. "Under partnering, all parties [involved in the construction project] agree from the beginning, in a formal structure, to focus on creative cooperation and work to avoid adversarial confrontation. Working relationships are carefully and deliberately built, based on mutual respect, trust, and integrity. Partnering provides participants with a win-win orientation toward problem resolution and fosters synergistic team work."[42]

Charles E. Cowan was one of the first architects of partnering during his time at the Army Corps of Engineers. He later accepted the position of Director at the Arizona Department of Transportation (ADOT), with the charge to bring the partnering concept to ADOT. He was recently moved to his current position for the purpose of bringing partnering to other Arizona State agencies.

Synergistic Alliances for Distribution and Marketing. If you can't reach a customer or you have a customer you'd like to sell more to—do what Dean Witter and NationsBank did: A subsidiary of Dean Witter and a Subsidiary of NationsBank of North Carolina will each own 50 percent of the new firm, which will operate under the name Nations Securities, A Dean Witter/NationsBank Company...Nations Securities is an independent securities brokerage firm that began operations in 1993, with approximately 400 Investment Officers, located at selected NationsBank banking centers around the country.

"Dean Witter's partnership with NationsBank is truly a unique alliance which is unprecedented in both the securities and banking industries," observes Philip J. Purcell, Chairman and Chief Executive Officer of Dean Witter Financial Services Group. "Dean Witter and NationsBank are ideal partners because we share the same values, are dedicated to serving the consumer and are leaders in our respective industries."[43]

Each had something the other could use. NationsBank has the flow of depositors. Dean Witter, a different and more profitable product to market to NationsBank depositors.

Coca-Cola and Nestle Foods developed an alliance for distributing Nestle's iced coffee drink in Korea. Coke had the channel of distribution and Nestle had a product that didn't directly compete with their existing products. Maximizing the marketing value you receive from any partner is crucial for alliances to survive.

Companies with sales forces consisting of individuals and organizations who are not directly employed by or directly under the control of the company are already in an alliance—one with their representatives and or distributors. These alliances consist of non-exclusive and exclusive synergistic alliances:

Non-Exclusive agreement—Steelcase, Inc., the world's largest manufacturer of office furniture and office environments, distributes their products through their independent dealer network. While the dealers have the ability to sell other lines and offer accessory products from other manufacturers to round-out their product line and better fulfill the needs of their customers needs, Steelcase will not sell direct, but only through their dealers.

Independent contractors—companies like State Farm Insurance Companies, demand exclusivity. In contrast, the sports and clothing industries work well with multi-line representatives.

"The competitive edge in the future will come not only from rates, but from the quality of service given the customer," observes Edward Rust, Jr., president of State Farm Insurance in Bloomington, Illinois. "Successful State Farm Agents in the years ahead will be the ones who make the most of their greatest asset...the personal, professional service that they can offer policyholders."[44]

State Farm refers to their alliance with agents as the "Marketing Partnership," under this umbrella, are the elements of the alliance (contract, compensation, renewal ownership, co-op advertising, and termination). State Farm gives their agents everything they need to conduct business and sells them other items to make it better. Part of this partnership is computer hardware and software available for lease, and because they continually upgrade the system, State Farm shoulders the capital investment costs.

Access is a key ingredient to successful alliances. Because they feel so strongly about the value of this marketing partnership relationship with the agents, State Farm executives go the extra mile to encourage partnering through quality communication. At their annual agents conference, all senior officers, including the president are available to the agents in an informal setting for an afternoon where agents can air concerns and get questions answered. This has been part of their culture for as long as the "old timers" can remember.

Jafra Cosmetics markets their cosmetics exclusively to women, and through women. They're quite clear about their positioning strategy and their market. Jafra is committed to their strategy of distributing their products through synergistic alliances with their field consultants. Pat Krupa shared some thoughts about partnering with their strategic alliance:

"Since most of our consultants work [also at another job], the access to new or potential customers is through business associates, family, and workshops she can attend monthly. The manager who teaches our Seven Basics of Consultantship, has a personal investment in helping each woman succeed."

"A well-trained consultant in our program will offer you an opportunity to learn about yourself, give you instructions on how to use our product, and she'll give you an opportunity to purchase it at a special value available to you for coming to the class. So what we believe is that the best opportunity for you is to try the product without pressure and without a demand that you purchase something. But a well-trained consultant will show you the benefit of using the product."

"No matter how busy a woman gets, she still has a need to get together with other women in an interactive situation. The busier the woman, the greater the relief it is to get together with something that is just totally for herself. Our method is relaxing, fun, informative, and saves time because she [the customer] doesn't have to go shopping to look for a regiment to care for her skin and body. And, it's with people she trusts. If you go to the store, you generally don't know the salesperson."[45]

COMMUNITY BASED ALLIANCES

Professionals and small businesses alike can reduce marketing costs by positioning themselves with a public activity and share in the expenses as well as the rewards. John Grace, branch manager of the Westlake Village office of Financial Network Investment Corporation, in conjunction with others in the local business community, put together an annual event called the Economic Forum. Designed to set apart his office from the look-alike competitors, Grace and his alliance, consisting of a local CPA firm, bank, law firm, newspaper, university school of business, commercial real estate brokerage firm, insurance agent and restaurant, host more than 200 clients and guests each year.

The forum, held at the local university, boasts high-level speakers who discuss auspicious economic concerns of the community residents in attendance. For example, in 1990, Dr. Robert Goodman, an economist formerly with the Federal Reserve Board and currently the

Chief Economic Advisor with the Putnam Companies of Boston was the keynote speaker.

In 1994 in a continuing endeavor to maintain uniqueness, in 1994 the invitations were printed on the only paper in the world made from post consumer U.S. currency.

The Sponsoring firms enjoy excellent name recognition, the ability to cross pollinate clients, to show appreciation and guidance to existing clients and customers, produce goodwill in the community, and receive leads from interested attendees...and conduct business. In fact, after hearing a cassette tape of the event and some limited discussion with a registered financial representative, one person gladly handed over an investment check of $100,000.

A successful, community based triad alliance, creating value for all involved, occurs annually in San Francisco. The 1991 event came deep in a recession, a time when many charitable organizations were experiencing greater than usual cash flow concerns. The event alliance consisted of the San Francisco Leukemia Society, Hastings, a retailer clothing, and individuals in the community who had collected donations. The individual who collected the most money, was to be named the Hastings Man or Women of the Year.

The person who raised the most money for the Leukemia Society in a five week period, had their photograph taken in a Hastings suit and was featured on 10 billboards (paid for by Hastings), throughout the community. Hastings, famous for their billboards, got involved with the Leukemia Society when one of their store managers died. In honor of him. Originally, the Hastings man was picked on charity donations.

Enter, Patricia Fripp, entrepreneur, professional speaker, and determined woman. After some arm twisting by Liz Hills of the Leukemia Society, along with the scent of victory, the vision of seeing herself on 10 billboards in her own community (in 1975, when Fripp opened her first business, a hair styling salon, she had dreamed of billboard advertising, but could not afford that luxury), and knowing she could make a difference, she became motivated to enter the contest. This was a chance to have her dream.

Fripp set the goal to raise $30,000 in one month—she picked that number because in the prior year, the entire contest raised $30,000. The community campaign was very successful that year, raising a total of $100,000. Fripp, met her goal. She felt great about making a valuable contribution while increasing her community exposure. Part of her overall business marketing strategy of being a motivational speaker.

How did they do it? At the first billboard, they had a party. The charity got the Mayor, Art Agnos, to proclaim it Patricia Fripp Day in San Francisco and issue a proclamation. The Leukemia Society also got the president of the Board of Supervisors, Angela Aliotto, to attend the party and present the proclamation. Mary Kelly of the Hastings Stores, saw to it that her company provided champagne and helium balloons—along with volunteers to blow up the balloons and serve the champagne.

Fripp bought T-shirts and buttons for all the helpers and had her National Speakers Association (NSA) colleagues write and sing an original song, "There's No Billboard, Like Fripp's Billboard" to the music, "No Business, Like Show Business" and ex-Broadway performer, Gordon Shearer, led the Fripp Singers. NSA friend, Paula Statman, wrote a rap song, "Give Me Money—Give Me Fripp" which was also performed.

Fripp had the event video taped, hired a Mother Theresa look-alike to bless the billboard and keep it graffiti free, and an Elvis impersonator to make a surprise appearance. By inviting all her contributors and friends, they were able to create a big stir on the street corner, attracting the attention of passing motorists. A friend contacted a popular local columnist, Herb Caen of the Chronicle and got him to mention Fripp in his column.

Hastings and Patricia rented a booth together at a Chamber of

Commerce event. Mary Kelly of Hastings brought a small monitor to show the video of the billboard party, and brought a miniature version of the sign. By splitting the expenses, both the entrepreneur, Fripp, and the corporation, Hastings benefitted from the Fripp's personality draw at the booth.

At Christmas, Hastings organized and paid for a catered party in Fripp's honor at one of their store locations where she gave a speech on "How to Win in a Recession" which was a great draw in the San Francisco community. Again she invited friends, associates and contributors, including the Fripp Singers and Fripp Rappers for entertainment. Hastings and Fripp gave bags of gifts to attendees which included, Fripp's Audio cassette pack, specialty advertising giveaways, an expensive writing pen, along with other premiums and bonuses provided by Hastings.

Fripp always accomplishes what she sets out to do and in the process, creates additional value for others who choose to participate. You may not be a Fripp, but you can surely do much more than you think—keep this in mind the next time you get invited to participate in a community event. Synergy prevailed, the Leukemia Society received donations far beyond their expectations, Hastings got the exposure they were looking for in greater doses than expected, and Fripp received tens of thousands of dollars worth of promotional exposure for her efforts.

KNOW YOUR COMPETITION BETTER THAN THEY KNOW THEMSELVES

A key ingredient to business success is in knowing your core strength, like Federal Express absolutely, positively getting your package to its domestic destination overnight and those of your competitors, like DHL Worldwide Express in overseas delivery. Select partners for your alliance with core strengths that supplement yours. This is really what partnering is all about. The synergy created by partners with complementary strength is what usually makes the determination between small and large success. One caution, be clear on each of your weaknesses too. This is important because one partner's strength/s must compensate for the other's weaknesses for an alliance to be successful. Partnering in this fashion provides a way to excel beyond your competition's capabilities by adding value to your products and services.

First, explore each partner's core strengths and then determine the differentiators of each's core strengths—blend the best of what each brings to the partnering alliance, remembering that both must share the core competencies of quality relationships and communications. Be clear on the difference between a core strength and simply something you do well. This "thing you do well" might be an activity that could be dropped from the framework or fabric of your organization and have no real effect. Conversely, an activity that if deleted from your structure would have a devastating effect, would be a core strength. An example of this would be Steelcase, Inc.'s dealer alliance.

The dealer alliance is their channel for distribution of the office environments they manufacture. Steelcase products can *only* be purchased through a Steelcase dealer. Steelcase receives information about their competition from their dealers. This exchange of information assists Steelcase in determining future strategies.

"They [the dealers] are sharing their success stories, which is very beneficial," expresses Deanna Wolz, director dealer alliances, at Steelcase. "They are working very hard with our particular group to try to link any success stories that they have in terms of sales, or think that they can directly contribute to the bottom line to world class performance. And, they keep asking us—they prod—they don't just ask and walk away."

"On Wednesday there are actually four dealer principals who are flying into Grand Rapids to spend three hours in the afternoon talking with the dealer alliance group about what it's like being a dealer, and letting them ask questions."

"Prior to that, last month we had two dealers, that used to be Steelcase employees, come in and spend time with his own staff talking about how I used to look at things when I was at Steelcase and how I look at things now that I'm a dealer, and how things have changed in an effort to try to help us better understand who they are and what they deal with on a day-to-day basis. Those dealers are taking time out of their own business."

There's a dealer that's full time participating on BPRT (Business Process Re-engineering Team). That dealer pops in monthly and sits on the team. That's a tremendous commitment in terms of time. They are doing this because they want to."[46]

Next, you must learn the core strengths of your competition and the core strengths of their alliance partners if it applies. "Know your competition better than they know themselves," says John Sculley.[47] It makes sense to know what the other people in your industry are doing.

One way to find out is to ask your suppliers. They may also be suppliers to your competition. Visit your competition—go to their place of business, phone them with inquiries or answer their direct mail solicitations. Always be asking yourself, "Why would someone buy from them?"

You need to analyze what they're doing right, then adapt it to your business. A customer survey is a possibility. Survey your customers as to what they like about your competitors. Next, determine what they are doing wrong, but (the survey can assist here also)—for heaven's sake don't tell them in a weak moment of proficient egotism. Keep it to yourself—profit from your competitor's mistakes! If you are thinking, "This is work!" You're right! Being successful is work—and yet it can be fun. No magic trick will make you a competent business person, marketer or partner but smart hard work can.

Now that you know what your competitors do well, maybe even better than you, it's time to gain new skills, technology, or competencies that will make you more competitive. You can grow these skills within your organization, hire the skills from the outside, or develop alliances with others who have the skills you need.

PARTNERING TO BEAT THE COMPETITION

You might have heard the old story about two backpackers settling down for the night when one suddenly starts putting his running shoes on. The other, in his sleeping bag, asked, "Why are you doing that?" His reply, "Because I hear a bear."

The one in the sleeping bag said, "Silly, you can't out run a bear in the woods."

In haste tying his shoes, the first backpacker said, "I only need to out run you!"

Some friend! This pre-partnering concept of only looking out for oneself is limiting. By partnering, they could have used their collective skill and cunning to capture the bear and sell it to a zoo, realizing a profit for their cooperation. How could you work with another to surpass an industry leader?

Donnelly Corp., founded in Holland, Michigan, in 1905 as a manufacturer of mirrors for the home furniture industry, now supplies mirrors and windows to the transportation market, and transparent coatings on glass to the information-display market. They currently manufacture 98 percent of the rear view mirrors for North American automobiles, have several automotive and non-automotive joint ventures, and synergistic alliances. Their partners assist them in being far ahead of their competition. They have automotive alliances with; Ashi Glass Company, Ltd. (Japan), Group Happich Europe (Germany), Leopold Kostal Gmbh & Co., KG (Germany), Lectron Products, Inc. (U.S.), Matsuyama Seisakusho K.K. (Japan), PPG Industries (U.S.) and St. Gogian Vitrage (France). They have also entered into joint ventures in the non-automotive arena with; Optical Coating Laboratory, Inc. of California (Electrochromic Technology Company, California), Optical

Shields (OSD Envision, California) and with Applied Films Laboratory (Donnelly Applied Films, Incorporated, Colorado).

The joint venture with Applied Films was a marriage of Donnelly's world-wide market share and Applied's production technology. Because of Applied's size, they were consistently ahead but didn't have the market share to make efficient use of their production capability. By combining efforts, Donnelly saved having to invest in production capability and Applied could become much more cost efficient. The result—a successful Donnelly Applied Films, Incorporated manufacturing thin-film coatings for use in the world electronics industry, particularly in the manufacture of liquid crystal displays (LCDs).[48]

Coca-Cola, finally waking up to their main competitor, Pepsi, decided to make some improvements in distribution through partnering. "It isn't that there are any problems with Coke's numbers," claims a Wall Street Journal article. "On the contrary, the company has emerged from its strongest decade ever. Coke's profit growth and stock price have been robust. Through an aggressive push abroad, it now gets fully 80% of its profits from overseas. And in the U.S., it has maintained a solid market share lead over Pepsi—41% to 33%—while deftly swiping Pepsi's major restaurant customers."[49] But the decline in carbonated soft drinks consumption is eminent and Coke has developed an alliance with Nestle.

The new company, a joint venture, Coca-Cola Nestle Refreshments Company is based in Tampa, Florida. From Coke came experts in bottling, personnel, and law. From Nestle came experts in marketing, technical research, and finance. Their goal—to be very profitable by the end of the decade and the world leader in their product category. Coke-Nestle was born in March 1991, when Coke, the world's biggest soft drink company, and Nestle, the world's biggest food company formed to make canned and bottled coffees and teas for a worldwide market.[50] Nestle putting its coffee-making technology together with

Coke's world-wide distribution system, launched its first coffee drink in Seoul, South Korea on October 1, 1991.[51]

LOYALTY AND DISLOYALTY OF PARTNERS

A significant issue worth exploring—the issue of not being loyal to your partners. Case in point, Shipley's Family Clothing stores, with 10 locations in Southern California. Levi Strauss & Co. decided to end its relationship with Shipley's, claiming they violated a policy that forbids resales to wholesalers or other dealers. "Levis accounted for more than 40% of our stores' business, and if you look at indirect sales...it stands for more," said David Fleming, president of parent Shipley's Industries Inc. in Huntington Beach, CA.[52] The end result—more than two decades old Shipley's liquidated and closed its doors.

Japanese companies came to the United Stated to invest in the American steel industry and formed joint partnerships. Japan brought to the table capital and efficient production facilities—American companies supplied the technology. Many say the hidden agenda was to help make the two economies so interdependent that protectionist and "buy American" policies would become impractical—only time will tell.

American steel manufacturers didn't think their Japanese joint-venture partners were being loyal in the summer of 1992, American steelmakers filed suit against them on grounds of dumping. To the Japanese, this action was also viewed as disloyalty. "Japanese companies went into the United States and helped rebuild the U.S. steel industry in partnership with American companies," said Kenji Ochi, then head of the Ministry of International Trade and Industry's steel industry section. For the U.S. companies to turn around and file complaints against those same partners is, from the Japanese point of view, unthinkable."[53]

You may not suffer the predicaments previously described, even if you are not loyal to your partnering alliance members...but then again you may! Loyalty is such an important issue—in any kind of an alliance or partnership where loyalty is built and earned. This makes your partner selection process even more crucial. If you are disloyal to your partners, you will most likely find them shifting loyalties and entering into partnering alliances with your competition and sharing sensitive information about you. This does little to assist your goal of knowing your competition better than they know themselves.

The bottom line is: When you select a partner to help you get to where you want to go—treat them the way *they* want to be treated—with respect and loyalty! It's much like divorce, during the relationship both are intimate, sharing the same bed and work together as a team—but when the relationship is derailed—both can, and usually do, fight simply for the pleasure of making the other's life miserable and for validation on being RIGHT!

PARTNERING FOR PUBLICITY

Walt Disney Co. stands out as the master of partnering for publicity. Case in point: Disney World's 20th anniversary, a month-long celebration in Orlando, Florida. *The Los Angeles Times* of October 2, 1991, reported that Disney paid for a number of hotel rooms, flight expenses and most everything else the estimated 3,500 visiting journalists from around the world needed.

NBC's "Today" featured everything from the items for sale in the 300 shops at Disney World, to Co-hosts, Bryant Gumbel and Katie Couric chumming it up with life-size Disney characters. This was accomplished over a two day period. It was reported that Tom Capra, executive producer of "Today" said, "We did two remarkable, good shows."

He was also quoted saying that NBC had a barter arrangement with Disney World covering "Today" show expenses: In exchange for accommodations, NBC credited Disney for providing "production assistance."

Local radio stations, 250 of them, devoted their "drive-time" programs to the celebrations. President Bush got in on the action—delivering a tribute to his Points of Light volunteer program at the Epcot Center. Reporters from around the world were invited to attend the anniversary celebration and returned to their homelands with stories of Disney World. The result was international publicity that cost Disney a fraction of their outlay![54]

Manufacturers who want to get some brand name recognition can take a lesson from Franklin Sports Industries of Stoughton, Mass. In 1980, their sales were about $15 million and increased to about $65 million a year by 1992, as the result of partnering for publicity. Did they do it with a multi-million dollar advertising campaign like L.A. Gear? No! They only spend about a million dollars a year on advertising. When they signed up Philadelphia Phillies star third baseman Mike Schmidt to endorse their baseballs and gloves, Schmidt suggested batting gloves as an unexploited market. President Irving Franklin *listened*. A glove was designed and sported the Franklin logo in inch-high letters on the back of the hand. Franklin handed them out by the dozens to pro players. They liked and used his product. The result was Franklin's name being on TV every time the camera was focused on the batter.

A similar story comes from the sporting goods accessory industry. Oakley, grew from a motorcycle parts/accessories company into one of the best-recognized eyewear names (behind Ray Ban) in the U.S.A. In the mid-1980s, they launched a program to give away thousands of dollars of product to key "influencers" an several sports. In the ski industry, many ski instructors were encouraged to "Demo" the innovative sunglass, along with specialty shop owners, resulting in immense popularity among skiers. In bicycling, the story was similar. In fact, Greg LeMond proudly wore his "Oakleys" when he victoriously crossed the line, garnering the 1991 title at the Tour de France. In 5 short years, from launching marketing campaign, the name Oakley had achieved worldwide recognition.

GLOBAL PARTNERING

World communication networks and speedy international travel have contributed to the Earth becoming a single global village. Leland Russell coined the term: Geo Paradigm. Globalization has become a reality. For those who have success in their forecast—the understanding of what globalization means to them, their business, and their community is apparent. It is absolutely necessary to understand how this paradigm affects you, if you desire to stay competitive in the marketplace..

Global trends do affect your business: the optical industry, for example saw metal frames dominating the international frame market in the early 1990s. The frames were influenced by either a range of vintage treatments or high-tech materials and design. How did this affect those in the domestic American market? To compete, optical dispensers had to know the trends in order to make their purchasing decisions!

In some cities, globalization has truly come to town. What are you doing to meet the diverse needs of your citizens? What is the current demographic make-up of your marketing area? Building a bridge to these people, your potential customers, may open new doors around the world.

For many, an off-shore market may be in their future—one that you may not even know exists. Who might be your foreign partner? Businesses are invading the American shores at an unbelievable pace. This could be good or bad news—depending on your point of view. Learn the export secrets off-shore business people already know and successfully execute.

Exploit the possibilities, L.L. Bean did—they opened a store in the middle of the trendy Jiyugaoka area of Tokyo—a bit of down-home U.S.A. Partnering with Japanese customers to supply them with that which is quintessential American, Bean first established a presence in Japan through its mail-order sales realizing $14 million in 1991. Bean plugged into a Japanese trend of leisure, two buzzwords "free time" and "Resorts" became familiar to the Japanese people.[55]

Ford spent $6 billion, two or three times what their competitors spent, developing a new "world" car named Mondeo. This new car, the first produced for the global market, was introduced first in Europe (Spring 1993) and will be released later, in North America. Ford's new offering will replace the Tempo/Topaz models in the U.S. and Canada.

Mondeo is a name created by Ford, its roots though stem appropriately from the romantic languages' word for "world." During the development of this new model, Ford assigned different parts of the car to Ford units having the greatest expertise in that part. In engines, Europe developed a new family of four-cylinder engines, which are available in three sizes, while North America developed new V-6s. North America developed the power steering, air conditioning and automatic transmissions, while Europe generated manual transmissions.

Prior to this, Europe and North America operated autonomously to one another, designing and building completely different models, reflecting sharply different needs in the two markets. Not only did this project bring the two together, but Ford also received two new families of modern high-tech engines, a new line of automatic transmissions, and capacity to build 700,000 Mondeos a year in Europe and North America. Ford expects to sell the model for a decade, with a "freshening" four or five years after introduction.[56]

"Global competition is transferring both high- and low-paying jobs overseas. Automation, which has boosted productivity but eroded the manufacturing job base for decades, now is penetrating the service sector. Major industries are shrinking, perhaps permanently. And cost-conscious companies are turning to a contingent work force—part-timers, temporaries, contract labor—to avoid soaring fringe benefits and to increase profits.

Many labor specialists fear that the four horsemen of the workplace—global competition, technology, downsizing and growth of the contingent work force—will cause wages to continue to fall, creating a nation increasingly divided into haves and have nots."[57]

This may well be the reality for the twenty-first century. If you are to survive and prosper, you'll need to partner with your employees to help you to challenge conventional wisdom like Chuck and Loralie Harris did. They founded Loralie Originals in 1980. Loralie the designer and Chuck the visionary, built their company into a $15 million business in just over a decade. As a manufacturer of women's formal wear, this Redding, California company was also one of the very first to penetrate the Japanese market. They compete internationally from their small Northern California city with the major companies in the clothing hubs of Los Angeles and New York. They attribute their success to three ideas: basic ability, faith, and family support. Loralie and Chuck understand the opportunities of the Geo Paradigm and are in pursuit of it with the assistance of their employees. All of the employees I interviewed, spoke very highly of Loralie and Chuck.[58]

If you select an global alliance partner, be cautious of your expectations. A partner with a low level commitment will rarely contribute the results you desire. Donnelly has experienced "less than anticipated" results from an alliance in Europe, while it was very pleased with a partner in Japan. Dwane Baumgardner, CEO, asked about the difference responded:

> "There wasn't the same level of commitment. You could see it very early on how the technology was being transferred. One partner wanted to learn everything inside and out, and the other partner sent only one or two people." I queried Baumgardner about his thoughts on dealing with unachieved expectations. He said, "You work on trying to take corrective action. Do everything we can to make it meet our expectations and meet their expectations, and try very hard to understand and get at the root of what the problem is, because maybe we're doing something that is causing the problem.

Fundamentally, you reach a point where there has been a change from the time you entered into the alliance to now where you no longer hold a similar prime objective, so now you have to split up the alliance."[59] Maryam Komejan, Corporate Secretary added, "I don't think we've ever had to split up an alliance but we have had to smooth over some rough edges from time to time. It's like a marriage."[60]

Continual upgrading and updating is paramount for global success, especially if you desire successful alliances. A regular search for knowledge is extremely important. You must know as much about what is happening down the block as across the ocean. CNN, Turner Broadcasting System, Inc.'s, satellite-delivered, world-wide news network has been a major player in globalization. Through their efforts, the entire world can be apprised of important events, as they happen. Even with the 1993 sharing agreement between ABC and BBC, CNN still remained the sole global news network. In addition to displaying world change for the global population, they have been a stellar example of keeping abreast of how the world buys.

South Carolina has been successfully in luring foreign companies because of their commitment to educating their workers. Along with their traditional universities, South Carolina educates full-time students in two-year technical colleges. These colleges are not based on a baccalaureate academic model and courses often change depending on the current needs and requests of employers. This is one of the main reasons the state enjoyed only a 6.5% unemployment rate of its 3.5 million residents during the early '90s recession when the rest of the country was experiencing substantially higher rates.[61]

In 1986, Germany-based BMW, realized a currency crisis and to protect their profit selected South Carolina (after much wooing) for the site of their manufacturing facility. Others European companies like Semens (electrical), Bosch (auto parts), Hoechst, Bayer and Badische Anilin (chemical companies) and Michelin (tires) have poured billions into this southern state since the '60s—they've definitely gotten their share from globalization.

As the globalization trend continues, look to foreign alliances. Be cautious—the possible pitfalls to an alliance with a foreign company could be unenforceable contracts or partnering charters, along with the cultural difficulties. The benefits include access to new markets, through obtaining difficult to find knowledge of the country you plan to target. You can identify:

- Local tastes.
- National and local laws.
- Necessary permits.
- A myriad of minutia critical to your success.

All significant to new market development and globalization. Ultimately, you are responsible for how much you profit or how much you lose as result of globalization. You can go it alone with increased difficulty, find a partner, or ignore the inevitable off-shore competition. Which ever route you select, you can be assured your local, national, and global competitors will be looking closely at this paradigm.

PARTNERING WITH YOUR COMPETITION

Partnering with one or several competitors at the onset may seem a poorly devised strategy at best, possibly even a strategy born in desperation. If you approach this proposition without adopting the partnering precepts talked about earlier, you could end up holding a tiger by the tail and wondering what in the world to do with it.

Andy Cowart was struggling to keep his furniture and fixture company alive in a construction recession. "Our sales were soft and the competition was fierce," said Coward. His Lexington, Kentucky firm, Cowart and Company Inc. manufactures high-end architectural wood products. Then a dream contract appeared—a contractor for Disney World asked Cowart to supply cabinets and other wood products for a housing development. The job had to be completed within 95 days, and Cowart and Co., with only 20 employees was too small to handle the job so quickly. Cowart decided to take a chance on implementing an idea he discovered was popular in Europe: Join forces with the competition!

"I was brought up to believe that the competition was the enemy," Cowart noted. "It was, he said, a dream project, especially in light of the current economic situation." He developed an alliance with three of his competitors. They divided design, manufacturing, and assembling duties, and completed the $2.5 million contract. This model, Flexible Manufacturing Networks, is popular among small to medium-size firms in western Europe. The philosophy was once accepted and implemented in America among nineteenth century farmers, but has lost favor over the years. The California wine industry employs an adaption—the sharing of some high-cost equipment among boutique wineries. Cowart's experiment was such a success that it has evolved into the Kentucky Wood Manufacturers Network Inc., a nonprofit group with 17 members.[62]

Two local California telephone companies, GTE and Pacific Bell, entered into a partnering agreement to block Metropolitan Fiber Systems (MFS), a Competitive Access Provider (CAPS), from developing a fiber optics dual communications system to insure the University of California at Los Angeles (UCLA) service in case of an emergency. The CAPS sole objective, as suggested by Paul Childers, network planning section manager at GTE, is finding ways to undercut pricing to local phone companies' major business clients.

Childers explains that local telephone companies are regulated yet the CAPS are not—this creates a major challenge for local companies to maintain their business customers, which allow residents to enjoy a lower service cost than would be the case without the large business customers. In an effort to maintain local business accounts, competitors, GTE and Pacific Bell partnered for a common goal.

Pacific Bell allowed GTE to lay cable within Pac Bell's boundaries so both could deliver on UCLA's request and successfully beat their collective unregulated competitor. This multi-million dollar contract was signed by UCLA, GTE, and Pacific Bell in September 1993 at a gala ceremony—cementing the utilities' hold on another of their profitable business accounts.

Imagine officials of bitter computer manufacturing rivals amiably swapping sales ideas. Seems unlikely? Never the less, there they were— executives from America's high-tech elite, companies such as Compaq Computer Corp., Dell Computer Corp., Microsoft Corp. and Sun Microsystems Inc., gathered in a nondescript conference room in Tokyo's Kojimachi business district. Greeting one another like old friends, laughing and swapping jokes before sitting down to lunch and exploring ideas about tackling markets and expanding sales—in Japan, that is.[63]

Intriguing isn't it, what can make such strange bedfellows? The computer industry officials mentioned above, knew that the adage "United we stand, divided we fall," which had a particularly potent meaning in their struggle to crack the what's often perceived as the impermeable, Japanese market. And for Andy Cowart, the cabinet maker—who'd have guessed he would share the pie with his nemeses, prior to his 1990 revelation?

This strategy, partnering with your competition, can be, if correctly executed one of the most powerful tools in your partnering tool box. Again, let me warn you there will be pitfalls that I'll discuss in the next chapter.

HAPPY PARTNERS, UNHAPPY CUSTOMERS

Sometimes partnering with your competition will benefit you but your customers might perceive the relationship will somehow hurt them. It may even border on being a monopoly situation, which you'll want to view with discerning eyes. Case in point is the controversial tactic known as "code sharing" which is used by the airline industry. This is the practice of one airline sharing their ticket code, effectively their name, with another based on a partnering agreement. The result is a larger network of flights for a particular airline and customers not really knowing which airline they will fly on any one leg of their ticketed flight. In March 1993, USAir and British Airways announced "The Global Alliance," positioning the alliance as "Two Airlines. One Vision." They announced that the alliance would ultimately connect 339 cities in 71 countries and offer "a standard of service unequaled anywhere in the world."[64] They're certainly not the first, other alliances include: American Airlines/South African Airways, Northwest Airlines/KLM, Delta/Swissair, and Air New Zealand/Quantas Airways.

The airline industry claims that code sharing is a critical link that ties domestic airlines to international partners. I realize this is an incremental step toward the inevitable long-term globalization of the industry but it is also, if not checked, an opportunity for them to project an image—something more than they really are. Customer complaints include: Buying a ticket to fly a particular airline and finding they must fly a partnering airline on one or more legs of their trip. Many customers unhappily board a twin-prop airplane when they believed they booked passage on a jet.

I remember the first time I ended-up on one of those 15-seat puddle-jumpers. It was at the Oxnard, California airport and I'm still not sure which was worse—my 300 pound seat mate pressing me against the window during the heat of a July day without air conditioning, or the guy in the back complaining about his lack of the first-class seat which he had purchased. This is an issue to consider—does partnering bamboozle or defraud your customer? If so, is it worth it? Partner not only with your competition but also with your customers—let them know up-front exactly what they're getting.

In defense of the airline industry, Continental Airlines Holdings Inc. claims a travel agent has four different opportunities to identify a code-sharing flight in the ticketing process.[65]   Also code sharing is a powerful tool for the airlines, enabling them to retain passengers for a trip that requires at least one connection. It also gives code-sharing airlines a substantial marketing advantage in the computer-reservation system. For each route, flights that connect on the same airline receive a higher display in the computer than other connections, and travel agents tend to book most trips from the flight display screen. American Airlines proved that the positioning did make a difference. When they originally developed Sabre, the computer reservations system, their flights were always displayed first until the federal government required American to rewrite its software to eliminate bias toward any particular airline.[66]

When people think about partnering, alliances are what usually come into their minds. While synergistic alliances are usually developed with outside business, it doesn't always have to be the case. The key to successful alliances is to always be sure that all partners are continually looking out for their partner's well being, the same as they do their own.

Synergistic alliances will assist you in beating your competition by virtue of the extra edge the synergy develops, be it local or global. Remember though, sometimes it may benefit you to partner with your customers to do things on a larger scale than you previously thought possible.   All the while you're searching for, and building alliances—remember to be fiercely aware of how the alliance will affect your customers. Without customers, alliances are of little value. Your understanding of the first leg to your partnering pentad is now complete.

FOUR

PARTNERING WITH SUPPLIERS

Many suppliers that didn't learn to partner are finding it tough going. Big firms are slashing their vendor rolls and working more closely with the remaining select few. Xerox has reduced their suppliers from 5,000 to 500, that's a dramatic 90% reduction. Motorola reduced from 10,000 to 3,000 for a 70% reduction, while Digital Equipment decreased from 9,000 to 3,000.[67]

If you think about it, those numbers are mind-boggling. To put it in perspective, think about the people, your friends who would be out of work if your company released nine out of ten employees today, or maybe just seven out of ten. The pressure is coming from industry's struggle to slim down and tone up to meet global competition.

As American companies shrink the number of suppliers, they are putting more energy into the remaining relationships, and are even willing to pay a premium on the theory that getting things right initially is cheaper in the long run.

What will happen to suppliers? "In the change, many suppliers will eventually fade away," predicts Richard Buetow, senior vice president of Motorola Inc. "No one can accept just sweat; you have to show results." Xerox has seen its reject rate on parts go down substantially, due to shrinking its supplier numbers. As companies enter into partnering alliances with remaining suppliers, they expect world class performance from the select few.

American business, for the last 60 years or so has functioned within the paradigm of adversary relationships —squeezing the life blood out of all possible—a confused belief, "For me to win, you must loose." Fresh out of school, in the '70s, I was frequently warned about large companies having a strategy of literally taking over their suppliers' business by offering orders at an increasing pace, one that would require additional capital investment on the part of the supplier. Then when the supplier was deep in debt, slow down or stop ordering—the supplier would then be in deep financial trouble and the large customer would buy a controlling share and own the supplier.

This enterprise of taking over a supplier, I call the "The One Large Customer Syndrome" because that's usually how the takeover process would start. Years ago, a major retailer was notorious for this method of business but for the last decade or so has experienced a downturn, they recently even had to abandon decades old customers. Business philosophies change, sometimes as often as a new CEO takes the helm of a company. Things are changing and finally some are taking notice.

TIME FOR A SHIFT

The time for a major shift is now! The cost of doing business is steadily increasing yet only in a select few industries' profits are increasing to keep pace. The way America did business in the past is not the hope for the future. The concept of partnering with suppliers is more a journey than a destination. Regardless, of how well you think you're currently partnering—you can always do it better! If you've not yet accepted this paradigm, it's time to take a closer look.

Your suppliers may even be the needed connection in marketing your products. Dwane Baumgardner at Donnelly articulated to me:

"I'd say something that runs through all our relationships—and I'll use PPG Industries (producer of glass) as an example of one supplier that we have a strategic alliance with. They supply us glass that we sell to General Motors, so they're a supplier, but we also depend on them to help us market the product. You just have to work close with them and pay attention. There are a lot of people on both sides that can work *cross purposes* if you're not careful. So, it is paying close attention to the relationship and keeping everyone focused on the objectives of the alliance, and dealing with problems on a very timely basis."[68]

Tom Benson worked for Chrysler prior to his service with Mitsubishi, as warranty manager in their service and parts division. He explains old and new paradigm partnering.

"The idea was to get as much out of the supplier as you could. It didn't matter whether he was going to make money or not. But the Japanese will not enter into a relationship with a supplier if they don't think their partner, the supplier, can be successful.

I began to realize that is a marvelous idea and bought into that idea completely. I've actually gone to suppliers and said, we don't think this is good for you so you need to change it. It is amazing the results you get because then the supplier begins to work like a tizzy. That was the big difference between the Japanese and what it used to be like out here."

In asking Benson about his move from Chrysler to Mitsubishi I was interested in knowing how difficult it was for him to change his paradigm about partnering with suppliers when he arrived and saw the Japanese operating from the "win/win" perspective.

"It was easy to change because it's the sort of thing that you feel inherently good about. When you realize the logic and the goodness—that nobody wants to be in this 'beat them down, suck the blood out of the guy,' it's easy to go to a concept where we can go ahead and develop a system where we both win. It's a fairly easy thing to do because it's inherently the right thing to do and when something is inherently right, it's a lot easier to move towards it."[69]

"Some men see things as they are and say, 'Why?' I dream things

75

that never were, and say, 'Why not'?" -George Bernard Shaw

MANUFACTURING/DISTRIBUTION CHAIN

By understanding the possibility for calamity to arise, you can plan and organize your partnering agreements to hopefully eliminate those dreadful occurrences. One of the best ways to guarantee failure is not knowing your supplier/partners. Knowledge of your supplier/partner is imperative for successful long-term supplier relationships. In today's unstable economic environment, you want the least amount of negative surprises possible. In contrast, you would hope your suppliers (and they will if selected properly) would regularly surprise you with innovations, new technology, and applications for their products making your search a bit easier. In my days of selling to retailers the question most frequently asked of me was: "What's new?" Remember though, you must treat suppliers with respect so they desire to assist you with "what's new."

Depending on where you fit into the manufacturing, distribution, and retailing cycle, your needs and possibilities will differ. If you're a **supplier to manufacturers**, look for ways to develop stable partnering relationships with your manufacturing customers. Some of the key things they are looking for are:

• Geographically desirable partners having the technological capability and financial strength to supply them with the materials necessary to manufacturer their products. A Los Angeles manufacturer of store branded disposable diapers told me that these two factors weighed heavy in their corporate decision process when selecting supplier/partners.

• Manufacturers want quality from their suppliers in order to give their customers the quality they want. David Slikkers at S2 Yachts believes that suppliers to the marine manufacturers industry are two or three years behind in the quality movement.

"As we're starting to try to get the quality of our product better in the eyes of the customer, not in our eyes, but in the eyes of the customer," He recalls, "We're finding more and more that the wrinkle in this process is that the deficient product from the vendor. I'll give you an example, it just happened yesterday.

We had a $40 to $60 thousand dollar boat, we custom order leather couches to be in our products. We open up the box and we find that there is a huge blemish in the side panel of the leather couch plus there are staples in the front portion of the couch—visible! So we called the vendor and told him this. He says, 'Yeah, we were hoping you wouldn't notice.'"[70]

• Excellent pricing, sharp and to the bone, and a willingness to make long term buying commitments. More so than they were previously.

• EDI (electronic data interchange) capability, assisting them with their JIT (just in time) material inventory needs. This requires trust from both sides of the partnering table as sensitive information is being exchanged, while allowing suppliers to better predict their customer's needs, and fulfilling those needs in a timely manner.

Manufacturers, your issues are that of partnering with those who supply you with materials and your desire to partner with your distributors and/or retail dealers. Making use of JIT and EDI is critical in this competitive business climate. You must find suppliers that have the technological capability to assist you in future product innovations and development. You want a fair (not always the lowest) cost and an uninterrupted supply of materials necessary for your production schedule. You want your suppliers to be an extension of departments such as purchasing, research and development, and production—assisting them to be more effective and productive in their daily activities.

"Trust goes through the whole thing because if you have a vendor who is very competent, very technologically advanced, you trust him," says Miles Gordon of FNIC. "When I say trust him—that they won't, for instance, ever directly deal with the client."[71]

Trust is something earned, not bought or taken, yet your suppliers can only assist you when you share information with them, in short TRUST is an absolute necessity. JIT and EDI applications will assist your *profit* by lowering investments, speeding up delivery schedules and maintaining a continuous flow of product. This is only possible when you allow suppliers access to the data necessary to fulfill your requirements.

You too, must give in order to get. In exchange for sharp pricing and extraordinary service, you'll need to give a multi-year commitment—something they can take to their banker to obtain the capital necessary to gear-up to perform. In technology and knowledge advancement you must assist your suppliers, as you have them to assist you, allowing each of you be as profitable and as far ahead on the cutting edge as possible.

If you are a **distributor or manufacturer's representative**, your desire will be to prove to the manufacturer/s you represent, as well as to your retail customers that you are, in fact, their partner. To be of the greatest value to both, as well as to yourself, you must be a knowledge and innovation broker—sharing all you can and not taking it personally when your ideas are met with a lack of receptivity. In partnering, you must always look at issues from both sides and never get so dug-in on your position that you are blinded to the *bigger picture*.

For **retailers**, you are or should be, desiring to develop closer ties with your suppliers to get the best product, price and delivery so you can offer your retail customers what they want, when they want it. You hope the result will be customer loyalty—your customers partnering with you. You too must give to get—you must show respect for those suppliers with whom you do business. This is one of my personal issues with the retail community as a whole! You too can enjoy all the benefits I earlier detailed as applied to manufacturers, you simply have to treat your suppliers the way you want them to treat you—as if you were equal partners. Think about it—each can *survive without the other—but not as profitably*.

OPENING YOUR BOOKS TO SUPPLIERS

I once worked with a man who was so paranoid, he even resisted sharing company sales figures with his sales managers. As I stated earlier, trust is a necessary component for true partnering to ensue. Many companies are resistant to take advantage of their suppliers' technological capabilities because of the same fear I just mentioned—Pillsbury Co. is not.

In the food industry, where success is often based on carefully guarded secrets, this new paradigm of openness has essentially not been embraced. Pillsbury, at first, wasn't too sure either but they discovered they stood much more to gain then they would have to give up—*they got it*! Pillsbury's hit list of benefits desired from more open relationships with suppliers included: savings from improved quality, better consistency, more predictable delivery of key ingredients and packaging materials, and a higher level of commitment and support for product development and systems design.

Pillsbury gets exceptional commitments from their suppliers, who will usually go the extra mile, whenever necessary to get the job done. Their suppliers also participate in Pillsbury's vendor quality improvement program. Pillsbury has a "Supplier of the Year Program," an Academy Awards event for suppliers. In 1991, for example, only six suppliers were honored (less than one percent of the number eligible) and the group was diverse—ranging from a blueberry supplier to the company that supplies specialty ink jet printing equipment.

"In the past, we purchased on price basically because we had no other basis for judging our suppliers' performance," says Jon

Christiansen, manager capital procurement at Pillsbury. "Now, we've designed a system to reward them for things like high quality and technical capabilities. While these attributes may be difficult to quantify, we believe that they represent our biggest opportunity for reducing our costs."[72]

Pillsbury shares the results of their twice-a-year vendor evaluations which are based on data collected in six areas: technical capabilities, pricing, service, quality/conformance, total quality and manufacturing practices and safety; with the vendors themselves, creating a stimulus for continuous improvement. Christiansen suggests that success depends to a great extent on trust and that's why they set up a system that didn't mount one company against another.

Pillsbury, in return for service and commitment has assisted their vendors with seminars, defining the road map for the future and the efforts have paid off.

"In 1987, 90% of our vendors weren't aware of total quality management and statistical process control. Today, [1992] 90% have had formalized training and are heading in the right direction,"[73] says Barbara Huether, manager of ingredient vendor liaison.

The results did not happen overnight—as I've stated before, partnering is not instant gratification and it wasn't at Pillsbury. They've been rating suppliers for over a decade and have been practicing TQM for about half as long.

Bill Wright, manager, vendor quality improvement says, "The commitment and trust required to make a partnership work take a long time to build, especially when it involves two large, diverse organizations. The key is to sustain the momentum that keeps things going."[74]

Trust is the link necessary for companies to take full advantage of all the advantages their suppliers have to offer, especially with technology in mind.

ELECTRONIC DATA INTERCHANGE DEMANDS

Electronic Data Interchange (EDI) illustrates partnering in the truest sense of the word. This cutting edge technology will transport businesses of all sizes into the next century. Currently many larger companies are taking advantage of the benefits, but watch out—even some independents are now jumping on the bandwagon. If you want to move more product through those factory doors—start partnering with retailers utilizing EDI!

EDI, for example, allows a manufacturer to track through a customer's system just how much of their product is selling at each of their customer's locations. They can then ship product based the stores' individual needs. This keeps the customer's inventory to a minimum yet always in stock. The manufacturer can also receive raw materials in a similar procedure, allowing Just In Time (JIT) supply to production. Each partner in the process has computer networks that talk to one another.

Caterpillar uses an EDI network—the system has reduced their yearly parts inventory costs by $10 million. Pizza Hut uses an IBM Information Network for EDI tasks and Filenet Corp's Workflo software for its imaging tasks. Executives estimate the $1.6 million imaging system will provide 25% productivity gain and 40% reduction in the amount of paper used.

Stanley (tool maker) takes advantage of EDI to create 65% of its orders via direct connections with customers. Kendall Healthcare Products estimates their benefits will include $1,000,000 in increased profits due to their pricing system, and a savings of $160,000 in reduced communications each year.

Bernard Marcus, CEO of Home Depot, tells his suppliers what's new if they lag behind—he started pushing suppliers in the early 1990s to utilize Electronic Data Interchange (EDI). Sears put its foot down in 1991 with suppliers, demanding EDI as a condition to do business. They offered a free $3,300 software system to partner with their vendors—meeting them halfway.

By refining ordering and delivery methods, partners can reduce costs in inventory investment, space necessary to produce or sell products, insure the flow of parts and materials reducing employee and machinery down-time, therefore, reducing overhead and becoming more competitive nationally and internationally. Oddly enough, EDI is not a new idea. PPG Industries, which manufactures windshields and windows created direct electronic links with the automotive industry in the late 1960s, but the dedicated communications links were too costly to develop and maintain.

Supermarkets are reorganizing their distribution to help fight the Marts (Kmart, Wal-Mart, and others). As the mass-merchandisers are offering low prices (sometimes lower than the supermarkets can buy the items) for a growing array of grocery items, supermarkets are trying to beat them at their own game by adopting more sophisticated distribution techniques. This can be critical because supermarket profits are usually not much greater than one percent. Adopting the just-in-time principles of heavy industry and tying new systems into bar-code scanners is allowing stores to develop automatic inventory programs, allowing them to compete.

Modell's Sporting Goods has embraced the capability of some suppliers with trust by turning over inventory control to them. From New York, they weekly transmit sensitive information to suppliers like Levi Strauss & Co. in San Francisco where it becomes Levi's responsibility to keep them at "model" stock levels. The benefit to Modell's is that the shipments arrive directly at their stores and the dreaded "out-of-stock" situations are essentially eliminated.

"Weeks—not just days—are shaved off Modell's reordering process," says Larry Brustein, executive vice president of finance. "We want Levi's, and any other vendor, to know as much as possible about our sales information. We want them to know what's moving at which store and what's not at another." "It's probably every retailer's nightmare to return from the stock room without the size or style asked for by a customer. At that point you have probably lost any future business with the customer. Ever since we went on-line with Levi's, this doesn't happen anymore."[75]

While EDI can assist in many situations, it's not a panacea—trendy fashion and yearly purchases could cause you some problems. On the up-side: *Corporate Cashflow Magazine* reported in April 1989, that a telephone survey by EDI Research Inc. shows that almost one-third of Fortune 1000 companies were either using EDI or considering implementing EDI within two years. *Systems Management*, in their March 1989 issue stated that EDI is more than an expanded form of distribution data processing. EDI provides a number of advantages for business, such as; increased productivity, reduced data entry costs, more efficient and accurate data entry, better customer service and improved ability to compete in world markets.

SUPPLIER CERTIFICATION

If you can make the cut—as buyers are shrinking the number of suppliers with which they work—you'll enjoy a longer and more rewarding relationship. One of the ways companies are making this possible is through a supplier certification system. Usually consisting of about three levels. The first is entry. This is where the supplier is non-proven. The next level is achieved with some successes in quality processes control and improvement, on time delivery (not early or late) and desirable pricing. It's at the middle level that a manufacturer sees promise in a supplier and is willing to assist the supplier with technology, helping the supplier to become more profitable and enabling the supplier to sharpen their pricing to the manufacturer. The top level of certification is achieved by a supplier when the above becomes the norm and not the dream. This is the level that gets the EDI and long-term agreements. More about this later.

The basic idea is to have fewer suppliers, because there is always a cost associated with maintaining a supplier relationship. Large companies are assisting their suppliers in quality improvement and cost reductions through their experience and research. It's not always a one way street, as many suppliers are now assisting their customers with the same concepts towards world class performance.

In a perfect world (sure thing, you say) suppliers would deliver orders JIT based on EDI ordering systems, complete and with zero defects. Not only would this save time, it would drastically reduce costs for all involved. Materials arrive on the receiving dock and straight to the production line—no fuss, no muss. This is the target for which many companies are shooting. Steelcase has created a pyramid model in their efforts to obtain the "perfect world."

Randy Johnson, director of purchasing at Steelcase says, "We want to be able to assure ourselves that the supplier is going to be in a position to give us something we've obtained from other places, but in an uninterrupted supply line. You want to have parts and materials here that are good and you want to have them here when you want them. You don't want to have to inspect quality when materials come in the door.

We're really looking for suppliers who have the capabilities of giving us the quality parts when we need them. There's a process we have to go through—we call it our Supplier Quality Assurance (SQA), where we will do a self-survey. We identify our suppliers that we want to continue to do business with and then give them the self-survey to complete. We review the self-survey and then go out and do a more formal survey on them.

As part of the supplier qualification process, either they will be qualified or they will be at some levels below the qualification.

Then, as part of the procedure, we will ask them to provide us corrective action and feedback as they've improved."

Supplier Certified Parts Process

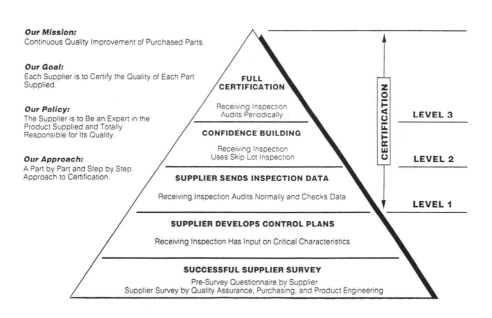

Our Mission:
Continuous Quality Improvement of Purchased Parts.

Our Goal:
Each Supplier is to Certify the Quality of Each Part Supplied.

Our Policy:
The Supplier is to Be an Expert in the Product Supplied and Totally Responsible for Its Quality.

Our Approach:
A Part by Part and Step by Step Approach to Certification.

FULL CERTIFICATION
Receiving Inspection Audits Periodically — LEVEL 3

CONFIDENCE BUILDING
Receiving Inspection Uses Skip Lot Inspection — LEVEL 2

SUPPLIER SENDS INSPECTION DATA
Receiving Inspection Audits Normally and Checks Data — LEVEL 1

SUPPLIER DEVELOPS CONTROL PLANS
Receiving Inspection Has Input on Critical Characteristics

SUCCESSFUL SUPPLIER SURVEY
Pre-Survey Questionnaire by Supplier
Supplier Survey by Quality Assurance, Purchasing, and Product Engineering

CERTIFICATION

As you can see from Steelcase's above illustration, they have three levels of certification for their suppliers. Before a supplier can reach the lowest level of certification, the supplier must prove their worth to Steelcase's mission which is, "*Continuous Quality Improvement of Purchased Parts.*"

Additionally, the supplier must show promise of being capable of fulfilling Steelcase's goal, "*Each Supplier is to Certify the Quality of Each Part Supplied.*"

When a supplier reaches full certification, their materials usually arrive in the back door and go straight to production, without inspection, as they have proven their worthiness for such a high level of trust. Periodic audits are conducted to allow the supplier to continually demonstrate their level of quality and performance.

"We want the suppliers to be aware of everything that's going on within the world class manufacturing environment," Johnson further adds. "Being a low-cost producer to Steelcase means that they're going to have to change many of their operations.

We want to have a partnering relationship with a supplier that can give us technical ability when we need it. We're not where we want to be with new products. What we want to be able to do is have a stable of suppliers that we can work with day-to- day. Whenever there is a new product, they get first choice. We go to them first because they have the ability to be able to produce the products.

I would like to be able to have our suppliers involved early enough in the product development process that they help us design products that we're going to get from them. They can tell us—this will work this won't work. We can get the overall cost down to a lower total cost in the beginning because we're listening to what they're capable of producing based on their systems.

As a practice, Steelcase is often times like many companies—you have a designer design something and you take it out and find somebody to make it. It's very difficult to find somebody to make something. You build a lot of cost into your product. So we want to be able to have the kind of relationship with suppliers that says, "We value your input, we're going to partner with you. We're going to come up with a product that we can all produce and we can all make money on."[76]

KNOW WHAT'S AVAILABLE!

I purchased a LaserJet IIP Printer from a friend who manages a local computer retail store. A week later I noticed a full-page newspaper advertisement by Hewlett Packard, offering a $195 Optional Lower Cassette *Free*, with purchase of the printer I had just bought. I went back to my friend and asked him about it. He was amazed, that when he dug through a massive pile of "stuff" received from the manufacturers, he found the free cassette offer. He gave me the coupon and I received my free premium.

Be sure you know all the details of your suppliers' return and repair policies. Find out about all the freebies that are available. Get all the point of purchase materials you can. Stay on their good side—you'll know more and get more. A mentor of mine, Lee Davis, would always say to me, "Remember the Three Great words that will change your life: *Ask for it.*" Let's also add, 'What can I do for you?"

Partnering alliances, relationships of equality, always yield greater rewards for all that care to be involved.

LOOKING INTO THE CRYSTAL BALL

The future of supplier/manufacturer partnering might look something like this: Mr. and Mrs. Smith visit their local furniture store and select a custom dining set. The Smiths select their specifications including wood type and grain, along with custom fabric. A deposit is given and the order is placed via EDI. The Manufacturer's computer receives and accepts the order, a production request is sent to the production department and raw material orders are sent to the wool and fabric suppliers' computers. There, the same scenario takes place, a confirmation and delivery date are electronically sent back to the manufacturer's computer. The manufacturer's computer transmits a confirmation back to the salesperson at the furniture store.

This entire process takes only a few minutes. While the Consumers drive home happy because they know the day the set will be delivered to their home, the wood is being cut and the fabric woven for their new acquisition.

An additional twist is that the Smiths had the choice of ordering the same dining set from their home interactive television screen or visiting the retail store for more personal service.

WHAT'S IN IT FOR ME?

Asking Randy Johnson at Steelcase if there was a question he'd like this book to answer, his reply was:

"What's in it for me? (as a supplier and as a customer.) Steelcase generally thinks it's giving suppliers something in a partnering relationship. I believe most people that go into this kind of relationship think the same way. I just wonder if we're really meeting our customers' and suppliers' needs.

Sometimes we at Steelcase don't know just how good a customer we really are. It becomes very easy to dictate to our suppliers. We want to be able to put ourselves in their situation and be the type of people others want to do business with. I wonder—in the suppliers eyes—how do we measure up? Are we a good customer? Are our suppliers motivated to do what we need them to do because we're a good customer?

If suppliers had to choose which customers they're going to pick, are they going to choose Steelcase? If so, is it because we're big and steady income even though we might beat them up? Why do they stick around with us? We've never seriously asked these questions about ourselves. There are some companies who are starting to ask this of their suppliers. If we do it today, it's rather informal—I myself, have never surveyed our suppliers."[77]

Johnson asks some very interesting questions. The most important is that of why a supplier does business with their customers. As with Steelcase, is it because of their size—realistically. I'm sure that has something to do with it. The bigger question though is that of, "Would the suppliers continue to support and assist Steelcase if Steelcase was down and out, if they were in big troubles?"

Because partnering is relationship-oriented, when both supplier and customer are continually doing more than simply placing and filling orders, the empirical value of the relationship grows. The level or rate of this growth will be a determining factor on how much value each places on the relationship and the possibility for continuance.

THE BOOMERANG ALWAYS RETURNS

Cost cutting has become quite a commonplace discussion with suppliers and buyers, but not all buyers are aware that the boomerang always returns. In the early 1990s General Motors Corp. commissioned their infamous axeman, their cost-slashing messiah, Jose Ignacio Lopez de Arriortua to lower materials costs from suppliers. Lopez demanded double-digit reductions from GM parts suppliers as well as ripping up existing contracts, throwing up for grabs the $50 billion GM spends annually on parts and materials. Rather than partner with his suppliers, he held a meetings to decree that GM expected cost reductions, period!

Lopez believed that GM's size could be used to dictate his expected cost reductions. Michigan area GM suppliers that I interviewed in 1992 were hurt and upset at the fact that Lopez was muscling them and were not very excited about fulfilling his demands. The critical element Lopez overlooked was that of being a partner to his suppliers and pledging his support in assisting them to achieve these cost reductions.

Lopez's departure from GM to Volkswagen AG, and the problems that quickly occurred; allegations that he snatched confidential GM documents which was reported throughout the media, including an article in the *Wall Street Journal*, July 26, 1993. To many, his troubles might have suggested that he was simply receiving back, the boomerang he threw out—you be the judge of that.

More important than Lopez "getting his", is that many suppliers, as stated in several *Newsweek* articles, cut back on their research for GM's needs and started giving their cutting-edge technology to Ford and Chrysler rather than GM. The boomerang in fact, did come back in purchasers' lackluster interest in GM products—GM paid the price for cutting Lopez loose. Additionally, some GM suppliers made the decision that they were not going to do business Lopez's way and either took their technology overseas or to other industries.

In contrast, General Electric Co. went after cost reductions differently, They assembled appliance suppliers at the Hurstbourne

Hotel outside Louisville, KY in November 1992 and announced "Target 10," asking suppliers for 10% cost reductions. The difference was that they pledged their assistance to suppliers in finding strategies for the reductions. This is quite important in maintaining trust, a core value in partnering. GE caused change and approached it as a partner.

It's okay to ask your partner for a better price if you are willing to help them find it. When suppliers and customers work in concert to lower manufacturing costs and the price reductions are passed on to the consumer, everybody wins. The more competitive a product is, the better it will sell and both the suppliers and manufacturers reap the benefits of greater sales and a secure long-term strategy of staying in business.

SEEK A HIGHER LEVEL

The next level of partnering with your suppliers is to do as Chrysler Corp. did, enlist your suppliers in designing and building parts, allowing them to find ways to lower the prices. Then, split the savings—the buyer gets a lower price and the supplier a better way to produce their materials along with a long-term relationship. The long-term relationship is a byproduct of their efforts to serve their customers' needs. Can this work? Chrysler did something that no other U.S. auto maker could do in 1992: make money.

Chrysler's answer to watching out for the boomerang catching them in the rear end is Thomas T. Stallkamp, vice president, purchasing. Stallkamp, is about as close to 180 degrees from Lopez as one could be. I believe the following quote will make the point:

"In general, the cooperative approach is the quickest route to better, lower-cost parts. When you start to see your suppliers as the experts, then they become valuable partners instead of a switchable commodity. You have to have some technique other than just bludgeoning to get some efficiency out of them."[78]

90

In conjunction with an employee team concept where engineers and builders worked together, Chrysler was able to develop the successful line of LH cars. Proof positive that clustering people together, pooling their skills and talents, creates the synergy necessary to get the job done.

ADDITIONAL TIPS FOR PARTNERING WITH SUPPLIERS

- Communicate by giving them unclouded expectations, providing formal feedback and ratings, and reward their performance.
- Reduce your supplier base by giving a greater percentage of your business to the remaining higher quality suppliers.
- Get upper level management commitment to supplier partnerships.
- The suppliers that serve you best should get the longest contracts.

FIVE

PARTNERING WITH CUSTOMERS

Partnering with your customers can take many forms and shapes. An excellent, but near extinct method is the honor system. Though not at every corner, the honor system is alive at Bart's Books in Ojai, California. When the store is closed, customers can still browse through, select, and purchase from about 1,000 used books found on a dozen bookcases mounted on the outside walls of the store. A carved sign on the door states, *"When closed please throw coins in slot in the door for the amount marked on the book. Thank You"* About this lost practice of community/merchant trust, Owner, Gary Schlichter says, "We feel good about it. It's a tradition going on since the store opened 26 years ago. Very seldom does someone take a book without paying. It restores your faith in humanity. I'd say at least 95% of the time people drop their money into the box."[79]

In 1986, Levi Strauss & Co., introduced Dockers which were designed for the soft-in-the-middle male boomers. Dockers became one of the fastest growing brands in modern clothing history, in 1993, after 140 years of manufacturing of dungarees. Levi's enjoyed Dockers' popularity, at the rate of nearly 7 in 10 American men owing at least one pair. This acceptance rate resulted in, Docker sales that surpassed the billion dollar mark, a feat that the company accomplished in total sales only after 125 years in business.

Rather than resting on their denim, Levi's then surveyed their top retailers. To their surprise, they discovered a defect, a cavity in their smile—poor customer service. Retailers loved their product, but had some caustic words about the company. Levi Strauss, swiftly set about making changes, taking 125 employees out of day-to-day business and forming 20 separate "initiative" teams to access possibilities. Based on the teams' findings, Levi's revamped its entire operation to better partner with their customers by becoming more needs driven. They committed themselves to develop closer partnering relationships with their retail customers. From a local bookstore, to an international giant, taking care of customers still pays off.

GET ON AN EQUAL FOOTING

Developing the third leg in your pentad star, one goal in partnering with your customers is to put you, your employees, and customers on an equal footing—allowing all to get what they want through respect for one another. Respect is a necessary ingredient to a relationship and the relationship I suggest is not one of servitude but one of caring about the other's needs. Work toward a mutually respectful partnership with your customers. Customers abusing your employees, cannot be tolerated—*the customer-is-always-right*, stops at the nose of you and your staff!

Employee respect and identification of customer needs are the philosophies that Leslie Wexner attributed to his success. As founder of The Limited Stores, headquartered in Columbus, Ohio, Wexner developed a total strategy and tactics for partnering with his customers by identification of a model person, representative of his selective clientele. For Wexner's spicy lingerie stores, Victoria's Secret, his selected model was Cybil Shepherd. He then developed the stores' strategic plan with her in mind. This is the successful method he continues to utilize in partnering with his customers. Wexner offers his customers what they want to buy in the environment they want to shop. In 1990, The Limited Inc.'s combined store numbers (including: Limited, Lerner, Limited Express, Victoria's Secret, and others) were 3,864. Increasing dramatically from a total of only 352 in 1980. The corporation's sales also increased from $295 million in 1980 to $5.25 billion in 1990.[80]

"To partner with customers, make sure you know what their needs are and work overtime to fulfill them—exceed expectations," suggests David Elliott at Technicolor.

It is important to communicate with your customers to find out what their expectations might be. Listening is a must! and to listen, you must ask the right questions. Ask empowering questions—the kind that open people up, allowing them to answer truthfully.

California Management Review mentions, Sonoco Fiber Products Division, as a company that seeks partnerships with customer firms. Sonoco is a manufacturer of fiber drums that replaces stainless steel drums in a myriad of industries, from cooking oil manufacturing to gunpowder production. Their ideal partnering candidate must have a "total cost" orientation. By focusing on their own costs, Sonoco believes customers are more likely to seek them out, recognizing the value they provide with their fiber drums and accompanying support services. These client firms are also likely to recognize that the benefits of joint programs and activities, are designed to reduce the total cost of operations. Sonoco believes that others, who evaluate acquisitions solely on "purchase price", and either perceive limited benefits from partnering relationships, or are unwilling to pay for added services, are better served by steel drum manufacturers.[81]

Tom Benson from Mitsubishi, suggests,

"There are two schools of thought in business today. One, is the idea of treating everybody as a customer. The other, is treating them as your partner. There's a difference between customer and partner.

Partner makes more sense. If you treat everyone as your customer you don't get quite the same relationship, it doesn't put quite the same spin on the process. The traditional salesperson/ customer relationship, I don't think, is the same in your mind as is partner. Partner is where both people are trying to accomplish something by doing it in a way that is profitable, successful, enjoyable, or valuable to both parties. That is partnering!

General Motors is trying to promote the idea with their Saturn customers that they are partners but I don't know if that's true."

"Synergistic solutions to their problems are different than a sales/customer, where you're trying to sell something or buy something. You're really not trying to reach a solution where both people feel that there is synergism here. There is something better however as a result of the fact that they are a partner. You don't have synergism in a traditional sales, selling relationship."

On how Mitsubishi could become a true partner with their customers, Benson responds, "That's a tough question, there's been a lot of books written on this thing, the so called a 'thousand opportunities to screw up.' There are several directions that you need to take. First of all, you've got to remember that traditionally the emphasis has been on the sale and not on the partner.

Where is the majority of the money spent today in marketing products? Particularly automobiles—the majority of the money is spent on the sell. Look at the advertising budgets of any corporation and you'll see how much money they're spending to...what we call conquest.

Customers generate income for the automobile manufacturers when they buy a new car. Compare that amount of money, the customer's investment, to what the industry is spending on establishing customer partnerships and loyalty over the long term. All the "relationship" dollars are being spent, in a very few months, before and after the transaction. There is some money being spent in the long term but it drops off very dramatically. I think we need to find some way to establish a long term relationship with the customer so that they will come back and buy a car again, so that they'll be more loyal to the product, because they feel there's some benefits for them to continue to do that."[82]

SEND IT BACK

Obviously, without the customer partnership, you're without a business. I recently cut up and returned my American Express card. Why? The service they offered for the price they demanded no longer provided me with the value I desired. Can you think of any companies in your industry that this example might apply? Might it apply to your company? I hope not!

Since sending back the card, American Express has not only sent me letters but also phoned me in an effort to persuade me to reinstate my account. Rather than partner with me when I was a member, they waited until it was too late. My mind was made up—they should have worked harder at keeping me! This is a great lessen to learn, especially when one can learn from another's losses. Don't make the costly mistake American Express made.

Citibank, in an alliance with American Airlines Advantage frequent flyer program, successfully lured me with the promise of free travel. I receive one Advantage frequent flyer mile for every dollar I charge, using my Citibank card. The bottom line is…Citibank delivers to me all the services American Express did and more, for about the same annual fee. The value-added feature I appreciate is getting the free frequent flyer miles. Hopefully the next improvement will be for an alliance to provide all of the above, but without an annual fee.

PARTNERING FOR PRODUCT DESIGN

There has been a paradigm shift, that of including your customers or end users of your products and/or services. Gone are the days of the arrogant Henry Ford allowing his customers to have their cars in any color so long as the color they wanted was black. Because of global competition, businesses have been forced to listen to what it is the customer desires.

Ed Howard of Steelcase says, "We have to marry the customer's feedback with our expertise, come up with an example and build it downstairs [production level at The Corporate Development Center]. The customer is going to look at it and if it's what they want—we move on it. We don't just paint it black because the customer said paint it black. We ask them what degree of black? Or say, 'Here's what we think might look even better.'"

In asking Ed what would be his advice about how others could profit from this paradigm, this belief system of partnering with customers. He replied, "Have confidence in your end user's perception of their need early on. Don't just use it as a validation point. Help them establish conceptually what it is they're looking for. That's the biggest evolution or change I've seen in 22 years in business.

Historically it was a validation, concepts were acquired from a variety of sources put together and then business would seek customer validation. You can track this to the old marketing business—they were validated with potential customers. Now the pressure is to let the client, who is accountable to use this thing—whatever it is—help you in how the need is shifting. How conceptually what you have developed is or is not working as well as it might.

This might sound overly simplified but it's really difficult for organizations to take career people that have historically not sat shoulder to shoulder with the customer and accept their concept of future direction. It's tough for the customer too."

"Take down the barriers—I perceive you as trying to sell me something at the end of this relationship. The best analogy I can give you: We were working on a bank in Atlanta. One of their senior officers was sitting there and he said, 'But Ed, what it sounds like you want us to do is let the wolf fill the hen house.' 'Who better to build the hen house if you're looking for protection, than the wolf?' I replied.

You've got to break the old paradigms of the supplier/buyer adversaries. The track you've got to break through on is coaching people on how to do it. Philosophically there's probably a way everybody can reconcile within the first hour of a discussion, but the methodology of the business process you would go through is where there's still a lot of rough edges.

What we try to impress upon the client is everybody at this day and age wants to come in and be your consultant because they're not sure what you want, that's the problem. As you bring in this partnering relationship you need to look at the credentials of the partner you're investing with.

Treat them as though you're going to invest in their company. What's their credibility? What's their proven experience? What's their financial position? How much pressure are they going to feel a year from now when nothing has been exchanged in value or received in terms of cash or dollars."

The construction industry, as I stated earlier, has done a great job in creating the methodology Howard was speaking of in their partnering workshops, where all who erer involved on a project were brought together to "iron out' differences, and plan strategies for successful completion of the project at hand.

Ford estimates that women are now spending about $65 billion annually to purchase cars and trucks according to a 1992 *Los Angeles Times* article. Industry analysts suggest that manufacturers cannot afford to overlook the extent of women's purchasing power. Flora Brooks, a Ford engineer, explained how the company's partnering with women influenced a design change. After one of the Women's Marketing Committee members caught her high heels on a seat track in the Mercury Villager minivan, the track was redesigned.[83] Slowly the American auto industry is asking women what they want, and whoever gets really good at asking and listening, will command a large part of the market.

INCREASING YOUR MARKET SHARE THROUGH PARTNERING

Classic Video, an independently owned retailer of home entertainment electronics, located in Newbury Park, California, has an advertising policy I believe is particularly effective. Their claim is to "match any advertised price." If you are a retailer, you might be currently making the same offer and that's great. However, they go a step further to partner with their customers by displaying all the major, greater Los Angeles area advertisements in the store. Customers know that they are getting a great price and a great service.

Next time a customer tells you how much they enjoy your store, business or service—ask them to put it in writing. They usually will! Display these letters in a noticeable public location. You'll be amazed how many you can collect in a reasonably short period of time. Regular customers will want to have their stories or comments posted—they will really see themselves as your partner—with their name posted prominently where their friends can see it. The result, a community bulletin board of recognition which will honor you, as well as, your partnering customers.

AT&T has a service called "Easy Reach 700" which allows you to partner with your customers for life. Regardless of where you move in the USA, you can take the number with you. This service is intended for residential use but can be installed on a business number. You pay a monthly fee to keep the number. This can be advantageous if you are a small business person and find yourself moving your office location more often than you would like. For an additional fee, you can order a vanity number of your choice—mine is 0-700-RIGSBEE (744-7233). This vanity number makes it even easier for your customers to remember how to get in touch when they have a need.

A '90s trend is for more people to be working out of their home. If this applies to you, you can use the 700 number for business—eliminating the worry of moving and your infrequent customers not knowing how to contact you later.

An additional idea is to use it as a toll-free number. When you sign-up you also receive several personal identification numbers (PIN's). You can print a PIN after your 700 number—customers can call and you pay the tab. Printing different PIN's on marketing and advertising materials will enable you to monitor what piece is most effective.

If you're a manufacturer, consider producing a poster listing the steps you use to produce the "Quality Advantage" or some other message you want to convey to the end user. Give them to companies that distribute or resale your products. Leave space at the bottom for your customers to print their name making it a personalized specialty advertising poster. Retailers will surely display the poster, assisting your positioning efforts and receiving personal benefits by using it as a selling tool in pushing your product.

Unbundle additional services from your basic product pricing. Lower your price to be more competitive and place surcharges on those "extra" services. Be willing to selectively let some customers and maybe even partners "walk." Firms that are anxious about potentially negative consequences should "pilot test" this strategy. By closely monitoring the responses of customers, competitors, and people within your firm; your management team can determine the viability of this alternative. If and when complaints arise, by remaining steadfast, you will be able to sustain the policy, although relations with customer partners may initially be strained. Additionally, you will gain some valuable implementation experience.

Remind your customers it's time to re-order or inform them that new products are available. A couple years ago I was introduced to an innovation in the automotive service industry—an electrostatic windshield. The sticker was placed on the upper left-most corner, reminding me when my next oil change was due. The sticker made my life easier because I didn't have to remember when my car was due for the next oil change. Additionally, with the Unocal name on the sticker it reminded me *where* to go for that next service.

If you are a retailer, send post card announcements regularly. The reason I suggest post cards is that it's less expensive than first class letters, and even less than bulk mail. An additional benefit is that you can keep your mailing list clean by printing "ADDRESS CORRECTION REQUESTED" below your return address, and the post card will come back free—do it with bulk mail and you must pay first class return postage.

I purchased a small quantity of envelopes mail order and about three months later I received a letter asking if it might be time for a re-order. It was a nice touch and I will most likely re-order from them when the need arises. Always look for ways to communicate with your customers and softly suggest they buy.

HIGH TECH

I approached the front desk at the Marriott's Desert Springs in Palm Desert, California to check in. The lobby was crowded with energetic professional speakers, as it was the site for the National Speakers Association's annual conference. The hotel, not quite ready for the number of people that arrived within a short time span, did something that was foreign to me. They checked me, and because my room was not ready, gave me a beeper. The clerk said that they were preparing the rooms as fast as they could and would beep me, when mine was ready. She suggested I relax and enjoy myself at the lobby bar until then. I took her suggestion and in a short while, my beeper was signaling.

The Cheesecake Factory is a restaurant in Newport Beach, California and is located in an exclusive shopping center. They purchased 80 high-tech pagers, that allow customers to shop while they wait. "It's very '90s," said Linda Candioty, vice president at Calabasas, California-based Cheesecake Factory Inc.[84] The pagers are unique in that they vibrate rather than beep. The diner's no longer have to rush to turn off the annoying noise most pagers make.

Marriott and The Cheesecake Factory are partnering with their customers by making their customers' experience the best through the innovative use of technology. Technology is important, but how you choose to utilize the technology, is even more important.

Another example of using technology to partner with customers for increased profits, is illustrated by service they offer at Oak Tree West, a delicatessen restaurant, close to my office in Westlake Village, California. They have "Fax-A-Meal." Bringing in off hour business, and hundreds of extra dollars a week. Local professionals and corporate staff who work late into the evening receive their "Fax-A-Meal" dinners delivered while they continue working. The restaurant does some lunches, but most of the fax business they receive is for evening and weekend meals. Some local companies have even set up house accounts to further expedite the service. It's not the technology so much as how you use it.

HIGH TOUCH

In a high-tech world, high-touch is becoming increasingly important. Pat Krupa, training director, at Jafra International suggests: "The women who choose to attend a Jafra class, [which are] conducted by an effective consultant, will experience enhanced self-esteem and self image through contact with that consultant."[85] Jafra teaches image enhancement through a high-touch method that assists their clients to achieve an absolute benefit—a happier life through image enhancement. Each Jafra consultant is deeply committed to affirming their individual clients' self-image.

Partnering with your customers by making them feel good, letting them know you care about their needs, and appreciate them, can be a profitable strategy. Recently, the Westlake Village office of Financial Network Investment Corporation (FNIC), held their first Client Appreciation Banquet. The theme was: *Objective Strategies for Smart Investors*. The evening was dedicated to the office's top 200 investors for their confidence in FNIC's ability to assist them achieve financial independence.

At the nicest hotel in town, the evening started off with financial advisors and various investment sponsors being available to meet with the clients. As the guests entered the dining area they found their pictures in the center of a one million dollar bill, identifying their seating location. The first class dinner included a champagne toast in their honor, followed by an evening speaker.

Clients called and wrote notes of appreciation, indicating how special they felt, and enjoyed seeing old friends and meeting new ones. Resulting from the event, the next day, a FNIC registered representative picked up an investment check for $130,000. Branch Manager, John Grace said, "If I would have known how successful the client appreciation banquet was going to be, I would have started it years earlier."[86]

PARTNERING FOR WORLD CLASS PERFORMANCE

Partnering with customers, and building relationships for world class performance starts by measuring for results. An example of this is Baxter Healthcare, a leading medical supplies producer. Using a benchmark, per bed measurement in determining results, Baxter, has determined that hospitals have a potential to buy $27,000 per bed worth of supplies and services annually. Its long-term goal in building relationships with their hospital customers is to get as much of that $27,000 as possible. Customer firms that reach projected goals are rewarded with an annual bonus based on their percentage of increment increase in volume. Customers that are having difficulty in achieving their volume goals are assisted by Baxter in finding mutually beneficial ways for the two companies to do more business together.[87]

Listening to your customer is also important for world class performance. Too many companies, those that cotton candy partner, listen but never act on what they hear. This has been a major problem at General Motors and has contributed to much of their decline. In contrast, Ford Motor Co. has a better idea.

Mimi Vandermolen, the highest-ranking woman designer in the auto industry, adopts a philosophy that is sensitive to the physical the needs of women drivers. Extensive research by Vandermolen and her staff has resulted in dramatic improvements in the 1993 Ford Probe. This car's innovative design was specifically created to compensate for the differences in height and strength of their female consumers. Its new design includes; less bulky radio knob and door handles, a lightweight trunk door, and a lower front end for a better view of the road. Vandermolen insists on a gender empathic staff. Vandermolen, says, "I've threatened to make our men designers wear skirts while getting in and out of a car."[88] With people like Vandermolen actively responding to the needs of women drivers, Ford Motor Co. does have a better idea.

Mitsubishi asks, listens, and acts—Tom Benson from Mitsubishi shares how they interact on mechanical and design problems.

> "It's a partnership between us and the manufacturer, but part of this measuring process is to give that manufacturer those problems that customers are having so they can take corrective action and improve the quality.
>
> We do this in a couple ways, first, through a survey and second, we have teams of engineers from the manufacturer come over [to the USA from Japan] to sit down and talk to our customers face to face. Then, we survey customers and if they have a complaint or a particular problem, invite them to come to our training center (we will give them a hundred dollars to come in) and talk to our manufacturing people about that problem. They get to come in and talk face to face with the guy that is in charge of quality control.
>
> People love it!! Also, we try to correct the problem right there. That's why we bring our customers into the training center where we have the equipment necessary to make the repairs.
>
> This concept applies to a limited number of people, but we do it strictly to get that face to face personality into it. If we can't fix it; if it's a normal characteristic of the car; we tell them right there. But if we can fix it—we fix it—or sure try to.

I was listening to a lady last Tuesday. I had been complaining about the noise from the windshield wiper on that particular model. But, here is this lady saying, 'How come with my Honda the windshield wipers go 'swish, swish,' but with my Mitsubishi they go 'clunk, clunk?' Those words were worth a lot more—here's the engineer that is responsible for this, sitting here and he all of a sudden says, 'Wow!' So they go back and eventually Mitsubishi wipers go 'swish, swish.' The engineers get that direct customer input which is really interesting to watch, and as a result—the quality continues to get better."

I asked Benson, "Do your competitors do this?" He answered, "I don't think so. I have never talked to anyone about it. I've had customers tell me I've never heard of this happening. They really do buy into the loyalty thing. And we do the same thing with customer relations. You can't please everybody. And, you never know in the beginning who you can and cannot please, so you have to try to please everybody.

You have to know that you won't always be successful, but will have some interesting turnarounds. One customer wanted to trade in his car when I first talked to him. Now, he's sending me market research stuff saying this car is so much better than other cars. I talk to him about every six months and he tells me how great the car is now, and he's telling everybody else how great the car is.

That's what we call 'Customer Management.' To some it might sound like a negative term, but customer management means that you manage all phases of your customer's buying experience. Not just sales management and not just service management—that's the concept."[89]

Ed Howard at Steelcase believes in helping customers solve their problems rather than just selling them products.

"We are very proud of the work that we have been involved with in meeting the health and safety requirements for our large accounts. There's a tangible need that the industry acknowledges but historically nobody has done a whole lot about it. We were okay, but it wasn't the front running issue for the industry. But by partnering with our customers we became aware of the fact that health and safety in the work place certainly parallels cost, in their concerns.

Health and Safety is finally getting a little more proactive. That is a very big issue for our customers, so here we are into an arena that at first appeared to be, 'Let's just make the furniture a little more adjustable and then the customer will be happy.' But that's not necessarily the answer—as the customer found out, and as we learned—meeting an end-user's needs for health, safety, and comfort requires a tremendous investment in good training.

You have to train people in what to look for. You have to train people in how to manage and adjust their own environment where they can. How to be aware of air quality and proper light. Those are intangibles to a point but they're core components of a healthy work environment. So here again, we bridged out of our historical, 'Well yes, this is a healthy desk—I guess, here it is and it's fine.' That's not what the client was really asking.

They didn't have the expertise to solve it either so they were looking for us, the all-encompassing environment company to come in and do a much better job in helping them be aware of the issues, help them identify services, if it's training or diagnostic services, to come in and work with them and then apply the product correctly.

The result for us and let's say, the telecommunication industry (the Bell companies and AT&T), is we both now share the largest installation of Sit-to-Stand working environments in the world. Right now, I think, we're up to almost 37,000 seated-to-standing workstations that are complimented with an extensive training program, and a user satisfaction program. So there again, it's that consultative arena we entered into.

A real-life scenario of what happened—five years ago, we sat down with customers that were saying something's wrong here and we're not really sure what it is. We don't think the furniture is right but I think there's some other things that are wrong also.

Through that diagnostic process, that consultative expertise of bringing the customer up here, trying different things, we recognized that first you have to start with some good training program and then you have to go through a good diagnostic program. Finally you get into user-adjustable products.

The innovation there is evident in all three arenas. But probably the one that has the most sizzle is the sit-to-stand work surface capability that you can help any of their directory assistance or computer-intensive employees work at their discretion, either seated or standing. It's an elementary solution if you think about it, but it is one that hasn't existed in the office environment since the beginning of time.

If we had not partnered on that, we would have had some concocted work surface and we would have tried to mass produce that thing and beat on our sales rep's heads and beat on our dealers to sell this thing. We didn't have to do that at all. We caught the wave of health and safety five years ago due to our clients painting that picture for us. Our dealers are riding that wave very successfully right now.

Our cost to market was reduced, our customer satisfaction was increased. It rejuvenated, realistically, 10 to 15 people I know on a first name basis—this partnering idea really has some power. We've got some converts that five years ago were skeptical.

We had a 94% acceptance rate of the first versions of the sit/stand workstation. Everyone thought, 'That can't be possible.' Normally, if we get a first prototype user evaluation of 30 to 40%, we've hit a home run. So we had to go back and do it three more times to convince our own people that it was so successful. The employees loved it. They said that all the time they had worked at these companies they never had the option."[90]

Ultimately, your goal is to convey the message, "It really worked well," to consumers. Sometimes we get wrapped-up in the sizzle while we hope and pray the production department executed their charge flawlessly. Throughout this book the central theme is to do more and be more, through partnering. Partnering can, and will truly bestow world class performance on your company by serving customers with innovative solutions to their challenges through synergism.

I asked Tom Benson of Mitsubishi to tell me what they are doing to make their customer's life healthier, happier, easier, and better—the ultimate value of partnering.

His reply, "Let me first say this, "We have a long way to go!" All of those evils that I told you exist in the industry—exists in the best dealers as well. So we're nowhere near being where I would like us to be.

But we have a good start—one of the things we feel we do well is—we have an extensive measurement process in place to make sure we know how our customers feel about us. It's a process from the beginning to almost the end. When you buy a car from us we immediately call you, within a couple of weeks to make sure you're happy. If you have a complaint, it goes back out to the dealer. There is follow-up on that complaint to make sure the complaint is resolved.

Every time an owner comes in for a warranty visit we survey them to make sure they're still happy. If not, we follow-up and try to resolve the situation—recognizing that we can't please everybody. Plus, we've had from the beginning of time, an 800 line where a customer can call us free and we'll try to resolve any problem. We spend a lot of money taking care of customer complaints."[91]

A final word about competing globally. David Slikkers of S2 Yachts has some strong feelings that American business must wake up and become aware of *all* their competition—he recommends:

"I think the course, on a general basis in American corporate or industrial manufacturing operations is that a significant movement is underfoot to become a world-class competitor or to be able to compete globally. If you're trying to sell products in California and you are in Washington or Florida, those states are not oblivious to what's going on in the other parts of the world. The West Coast is being invaded by the Asian companies, and the East Coast is being invaded by the Europeans, and it's even crossbreeding all the way across the Country, and there's no boundaries. So, if you've made a commitment to produce your product globally, you will have international competition. In international competition you will find yourself having to realign what you do to be globally competitive, not just nationally."

I asked Slikkers what S2 Yachts is doing to compete globally.

He answered, "Several things, first of all, we're trying to move much closer to our end customer. We believe that quality of products is defined as meeting or exceeding the customer's expectation—that's the definition we use. We don't try to come up with some type of flowery description of what quality is.

Quality is real simple. Does it meet or exceed a customer's expectation? In essence we get into a vendor-customer relationship and we're taking it all the way to the end customer. We have a distribution connection but temporarily, we're trying to bypass that in our dialogue with the end consumer. We don't believe we're getting strong enough feedback from our distribution network so we have chosen to go directly to the customer.

Every week we get in warrants and registrations from products that were sold across the nation. The very next week, a person from one of the following areas: quality assurance, engineering, or manufacturing call these customers. We're trying to make sure the product is living up to expectations. the customer has just spent anywhere from $75,000 to $500,000 on one of our products. That's a substantial amount of money."[92]

The reason the calls are not made from sales or customer service is that the callers represent the areas of the company which are closest to the actual building of the yachts, and have the power to make the necessary changes for improvement—just like with the Mitsubishi example. The ones responsible, must face the customers rather than enjoy the traditional insulation. To compete at the world class level, all in your company, from the mail room to the board room, must be as close to your customers as possible.

SIX

PARTNERING WITH EMPLOYEES

Employee partnering is like sunlight shinning through cut crystal—the light is refracted in many directions revealing color, beauty, and complexity. In it's purest form, partnering with employees is allowing and assisting people to become as effective a worker and human being as they possibly can. Business cultures range from achievement based, where creativity is rewarded and failure is an accepted cost in risk taking and innovation to dependency based, which is nonparticipative and hierarchically controlled. The culture that partnering embraces is that of achievement, and adds the element of *encouraged cooperation and stewardship*, seeking a higher level of results through internal integration and employee/management alliances.

Springfield Remanufacturing Corp. (SCR) in Springfield, Missouri has proven through performance that partnering with employees is a sound fiscal policy. Jack Stack, President and CEO, along with the employees have taken the company from a loss of $60,488 in 1983, to pre-tax earnings of $2.7 million in 1986. By 1991, they had annual sales totaling $70 million.

Stack reports four rules he uses to partner with his employees for performance, productivity, and profits:

- The most efficient, most profitable way to operate a business is to give everybody a voice in saying how the company is to run and a stake in the financial outcome—good or bad.
- The only way to be secure is to make money and generate cash.

Everything else is a means to that end.
- Make the system, the policies, and how things are done logical.
- Create and distribute wealth.[93]

Stack believes his real business is education, in fact SRC is constantly starting new businesses as fast as they can get them running. The businesses are run by SRC employees who have received their education from the company. By partnering with employees, SRC has enjoyed brisk growth and profits. You too, can enjoy this kind of success by developing the fourth leg (employee partnering) of your partnering pentad.

WORKPLACE DYNAMICS

In any business, it's the relationship between the employees and management that create the dynamics of the workplace. Leaders who endeavor to partner with their employees by viewing them as the company's greatest asset will establish a company culture of empowerment. This culture controls flexibility, initiative, trust, and energy levels, which dictate overall profitability and success.

John Funkhouser, President of Coeur Labs in Raleigh, North Carolina learned that trust was the key to productivity. Coeur Labs, a surgical equipment company was losing money when Funkhouser stepped in. Funkhouser recalls, "When I got here, there was very little trust between management and the production staff." His biggest challenge in partnering with the company employees was to convince them that he really cared about them. He needed them to "get it" that unlike his predecessors, he wanted the employees to prosper along with the company.

Early on, Funkhouser went outside for help in changing the company culture. He turned to successful entrepreneur and author, Robert Roskind. Several employees told Roskind that their quotas were too high, so he went about getting their quotas reduced. Roskind shared, "As soon as they felt love from management, they were able to, without strain or effort, produce way past the quotas."

Funkhouser confirms the payoff to partnering with his employees followed. Morale and productivity soared—sales increased 35% and the company is also leaner. A smaller work force (17) of motivated employees have replaced a larger group (24) of unhappy ones. Productivity has increased from 65% of capacity to 100%, all from building bridges of communication.[94]

Companies seeking the Baldrige award already know that a sixty-three percent weight is placed, for consideration of this tribute, on criteria relating to how a company utilizes their employees and activities that employees have substantial control over. Human resource development and management accounts for 15%, quality and operational effectiveness is 18%, and customer focus and satisfaction is a whopping 30%.

PepsiCo Inc. of Purchase, New York, is quite innovative in their efforts to assist their headquarter employees in reaching new heights of productivity. They created the first concierge in American business—PepsiCo employee, Andy King, holds the title. King does everything from arranging to get an employee's roof fixed, car serviced, to planning a child's birthday party or a wedding-anniversary getaway. PepsiCo embraced this ultimate employee-benefit as a result of a company survey that revealed employees were stressed out and had no free time for personal errands.

PepsiCo sees this implementation as a theoretical advantage to productivity. Company benefits include: reducing absenteeism and limiting the amount of time on the job employees devote to personal affairs. Best of all, this concierge service is not only available to those in the executive suite but to all 800 employees at the 144-acre headquarters facility.

Companies are changing expectations of their employees, S2 Yachts is one of them. They operated from a culture of end-line inspection which did not empower employees to be responsible for their work.

Inspectors could not catch defects that were in the bowels of a yacht.

"It gets down to what's an acceptable defect level as far as nurses dropping babies on the hospital floor," asks President, David Slikkers: "For too long we have accepted nonperformance. Nonperformance is defined as being responsible for your work. When I say nonperformance, I'm not saying he didn't work hard, and I'm not saying he only worked 4 hours out of the 8. We're now defining nonperformance as being, someone that isn't responsible for safety, or isn't responsible for his work station. Nonperformance could be that he didn't build it to the specifications. We're putting a much tighter definition, but also a broader definition.

We've gone to a point now where we're removing 'traditional' inspection. Within our own company we're moving toward a vendor-customer relationship from department to department. 'Okay, Pete, you're going to pass it on to Joe. Joe has the right to refuse your parts if they're not done right, and if Joe refuses those parts, you've got to make them right. That's your responsibility, to make them right.' So, there's a lot of work going on to make sure that it's done right the first time."

"The consumer base of the '90s is no longer going to pay for our gross inefficiencies. We can't get paid for being dumb. In the '70s and '80s, yeah, maybe that was possible, but not today."[95]

Remember, in expecting more, you must give more in partnering. People can work where they please, indentured servitude is a thing of the past. Companies that realize this, like PepsiCo, appear to have better and longer relationships with their employees.

"Our definition of a partner is anyone that we can do more with together than we can individually, in as far as mutual best interest to work together." Declared Dwane Baumgardner of Donnelly. He continued, "Quoting a statement of John [Donnelly, founder], 'Why does any one of us work at a company?' Why does anyone decide to join Donnelly?

The obvious reason must be they believe they can do better

working at Donnelly than they could do working by themselves. If they didn't, everyone would be working by themselves. There's a strong belief that working together within the confines of the company, we can do better—you form a bond when you do that. The company—however you define that—is bringing everyone together, making a commitment to each of the constituents of the company."[96]

"Real manager, means that they work with other people," declares Miles Gordon of FNIC. "If you're being a good manager you can't have a real big ego." "To work with somebody else you have to be able to get along. Real super high ego people have a problem with that because they think everything should focus on them, whereas in our firm we focus on other people. The better you do in our firm, the less your ego." "The classic line I always use in a meeting is, 'Ladies and Gentlemen, leave your egos at the door, we're here to share ideas not to give discussion on how great we are.' That seems to work pretty well."[97]

State Farm Insurance is partnering with their employees in offering security, they have never had a lay-off and managers are not hired from outside the company. State Farm has, since the 1940s, also provided an automatic cost of living adjustment (without union pressure) to all its employees. This creates trust dynamics, so important to partnering success. Adlai H. Rust, president at State Farm (1954-58) believed:

"Our greatest asset is not in the balance sheet. It is in the personnel of State Farm."

PARTNERING TO GET EMPLOYEES

Technicolor, Inc. in North Hollywood, California, the world's largest producer of video film and duplicator of theatrical filmed entertainment, moved in a unique twist; resulting from the 1992 Los Angeles riots. Less than a week after the riot flashpoint, President, Tom Epley, in a May 4, 1992 interoffice correspondence to employees, titled

Commitment to Change, stated, "Technicolor's management has made a commitment of time, ideas, and resources leading towards *permanent solutions*"—Technicolor was true to their word.

They hired Vicky Salazar, an inner city resident, to head up a program, "of giving people an opportunity." Salazar was quickly hired and trained to interview—in turn, she hired 24 people from South Central Los Angeles to commute daily (first shift leaves at 4:30 am and returns at 5:50 pm), 40 miles each way to Technicolor's suburban video duplication facility in Newbury Park.

David Elliott, senior vice president and chief administrative officer, suggests that partnering, in the above context is, "Joining two parties together for positive change." In his office with all the trappings of "the good life," talking to Elliott about this approach to making a difference and getting dependable employees, it was certain to me, that his statements were coming from the heart. I believe that's why he rode in the van the first day (at 4:30 am) with the new employees on their journey to possibilities (Newbury Park).

Elliott, who refers to the riots as civil unrest, said, "It's the first in a series, if we don't do anything." While Los Angeles was still smoldering, Epley and Elliott decided to make a difference—they did something.[98]

As a post script to the story, a year later I spoke with Elliott about the success of the program. He said, "I couldn't be happier."

Thousands of miles away, in Philadelphia, people are waiting at the Fern Rock train station which links the regional rail and the city subway systems. Much earlier than the traditionally attired business professionals, inner city residents like Sam Saulsbury, a food service worker in the Prudential Insurance Co. of America building, are reverse commuting. Saulsbury is heading to the suburban Fort Washington Office Center, a tree-lined corporate campus about 10 miles away.

This job and about 145 others, would not have been possible before the No. 201, a dedicated bus route, began connecting the train and the corporate campus. "We've been told in no uncertain terms: If it weren't for the bus, these people wouldn't be employed," says Charles Webb, manager of route and service planning for Philadelphia's transportation system. According to Alan Hughes, from 1976 to 1986, two-thirds of the employment growth in the nation's largest metropolitan areas, has occurred outside the central city. Hughes co-wrote and reported these findings in a study for the Urban Institute in Washington.[99]

The 201 was launched because companies in the corporate campus financially underwrote the bus. Not as a social program, but because of need. The local labor pool had dried up, and the employers knew people in the center city wanted jobs. They pitched in $7,500 and within six months, the line was paying for itself, not needing another cent of private money. Employers and employees see this solution to both of their needs and as a big "win-win" for everybody. Saulsbury, and his wife are saving their funds to build a house—one that's close to his work. These win-win activities create a strong bond. Both the employer and employee realize the relationship would not have been possible, had they both, not been willing to stretch.

HIDDEN PRICES FOR NOT PARTNERING

Both Bill Gore of the famed Gore-tex waterproof fabric, and the late Sam Walton, founder of Wal-Mart, the nation's largest retailer, always referred to employees as associates. Putting them on a higher plain, more as a partner. Your associates/employees are crucial to the success of any business. If they're treated poorly, your employees can devastate your career or even your business.

Scorned employees do things as radical as coming back and shooting their boss, to subtle things like, throwing large orders in the shredder, intentionally shipping out defective products, or misplacing confidential documents. If you carefully search your past, you most likely have been guilty of this, to some degree.

Today, I can clearly remember being 19 years old and loading trucks

117

for a variety store distribution center in Southern California. The culture of this company was adversarial between management and labor. In the extreme heat of summer, when tempers were high, I witnessed fellow employees seeking revenge against management by placing (actually throwing) the boxes of glassware on the bottom rows inside the trailers and then stacking heavy items above.

The cost of these acts surpassed the cost of the broken glassware, and represented lost opportunity for the stores. They couldn't sell what arrived damaged. Along with the return shipping, and paperwork costs, this employee sabotage was expensive to the company. The employees knew their carelessness would eventually reflect on the management, for whom they had little respect.

Remember the Movie *9 to 5*? Dolly Parton and company went to extremes with their dictatorial boss. They bound and kidnaped him, then ran the office in a more humane style in his absence. At the end the boss even got transferred out of the country. This was fiction but I'm sure it had a nonfiction origin. I suggest you make your employees part of the team—the first string. Then be ready to enjoy more productivity from their efforts.

The Chicago flood in April 1992, devastated 200 downtown buildings and could have been avoided. Upon learning that the city Transportation Department had known about the severity of the problem for at least a month prior to the disaster, Mayor Richard Daley discharged a high-ranking official. It was estimated that the repair would have cost about $10,000. Instead of ordering the job repaired on an emergency basis, it was put out through the regular competitive bidding process. Somewhere, an empowered employee could have made a different decision. The fired official may have been a political scapegoat, but the message was sent to city management—the message of accountability!

Examples are numerous of what could have, or might have resulted, had employees been trained, empowered, and encouraged to take a risk—in making a potentially expensive decision that they know would save the company or city, many more times the cost of implementing their decision. When this sort of culture becomes part of a business or organization, employees will have opportunities to build confidence and experience.

Your people make the difference in productivity/cost and quality which results in the ultimate value you are able to offer your customers. Since value is truly what today's customers desire, remember your employees are the first line on customer satisfaction and the perceived value of your products or services. Additionally, every person in your employ should be considered part of the marketing department because their interaction with the general public, and specifically with your customers, will have an influential impact on your positioning strategy. They are the determining factor in how your customers perceive your company. Subconsciously, we're all saying, "The conversation I'm having with myself about you, is my only reality about you." Let's face it, all businesses leaders that desire to be successful, want their current and potential customers to have great conversations with themselves about the business on question!

INCREASED PRODUCTIVITY THROUGH PEOPLE POWER

The Western Electric Company, Hawthorne Works, Chicago in a study (late 1920s and early 1930s) reported by Harvard, detailed that American workers did not leave their personal concerns at home but rather, brought their problems to work. It was also discovered that employees became much more productive when they had some say or control over the issues at work that affected them.[100] To market your goods, and be competitive in production costs—productivity through people power is essential.

Amgen Inc. in Thousand Oaks, California, a hypergrowth leader in biotechnology, posted total revenues of $2.5 million in 1988; $99.4 million in 1989; $298.7 million in 1990, $682 million in 1991, and

$1,093 million in 1992.[101]   It was reported in a *FORTUNE* article that, "Any employee can attend any meeting, any time, with cross-departmental discussion actively encouraged."[102]   Interviewing some of their employees, I found this to be true, the only exception was certain proprietary research. This, the including of employees, is part of the culture that made something possible that no other company in their industry was able to accomplish. They shipped $50 million worth of Neupogen (an immune system stimulant), all over the U.S. within two business days after receiving FDA approval to market the drug.[103]

Amgen also began a wellness program for their over 2000 employees in 1993. In a research paper, submitted to me by Lauren Leonardo, she said the following about the program:

"According to Karen Evans, the Staff Services Administrator at Amgen, the company was going to make the top floor of their multi-purpose building a recreation area for the employees, but they did not want the employees just sitting around. So they put in meeting rooms instead. When the meeting rooms were completed they had 3,500 square feet of space left over, so then they decided to put in their own gym. The facility houses top of the line equipment, free weights, an aerobic room, and complete locker rooms. The facility is managed by Office Aerobics, a third party.

The facility isn't free to Amgen's employees, but almost. For those that join, $20 is deducted each month from the employee's paycheck. At the end of the year, however, the employee is reimbursed $200 for Personal Improvement, leaving the $40 balance as the only cost to the employee. In addition, Amgen sponsors an incentive program for those who actually participate. Every time an employee does aerobics or uses any piece of equipment for 20 minutes, the employee receives a Fitness Dollar. The employee accumulates these Dollars and then can use the Dollars to "buy" fitness logo items, such as water bottles, t-shirts, duffle bags, watches, etc...

What's Amgen's philosophy?   According to Ms. Evans,

"Healthy employees make better employees." They feel that their employees have both physical and social needs, and their exercise facility and programs are designed to assist in fulfilling those needs."[104]

Additionally, they have recently opened a child care center which enables the staff to conveniently visit their children at lunch or whenever they want. Visiting Amgen, I noticed parents walking around with their children following closely behind. They have a family oriented culture and the children, being pulled around in the child care center's six-kid carts, stop even executive meetings (to watch the children) when they pass by. Amgen's caring for all the staff members is evident—even to the local community. All of this helps to motivate the employees "to get the job done."

At Cascade Engineering, a Grand Rapids, Michigan injection molder of plastic products, a group of employees proved they could make a difference if management allowed them to act on their beliefs. The Equachair line (where chair seats were molded) was the least desirable place to work in the plant. Employees rotated turns working on the line. It was hot, dusty and hard work. Dave Barrett, upon taking over as plant manager, had the Equachair line employees approach him with an idea.

Dave recalls, "In the first place we had horrendous external returns from the line. We were even getting high returns on good product and the cost of receiving it back was a heavy penalty. So it's significant to our cost of quality program. The Equachair employees approached me with the team concept as a way to improve quality. They also wanted to select the people to work on the line.

Additionally, We had a horrendous number of cases of carpal tunnel. I was concerned. I said, 'Let's do it. Let's try it. It can't get any worse.' There were enough people at that time, 8 people per shift, 32 total. Now we're down to six per shift—a labor reduction because of their efforts, not because of mine.

By establishing team leaders and regular meetings, slowly improvements began. We still had a reject problem. Interestingly enough, right off the bat, our carpal tunnel went to zero. Today, we've got people wanting to get on the team but there's no openings. The teams went through training and would actually select problems and work on them as they we were learning the problem solving process. We resolved major issues with dust, inventory control, sanding, trimming, and painting all by using the team involvement approach."

"You really allowed the employees to take control when they asked for it," I asked Dave? He replied, "You have to. It's one of the failures we had with quality circles and with self-managed teams. I really shouldn't say fail. We learned some valuable lessons.

Dave Kurr, scheduler for the north plant was a key player in the whole thing. He was assigned to be, the fire of the EQUA chair and when there was a problem, to try to work with the painter. For awhile, he became 'Mr. EQUA.' He was the one that really kept the group meeting and not giving up, even though they didn't get everything they wanted. I would tell them to just keep meeting, make small improvements and don't go in there with attitude that if they didn't get something they want then that's it, 'we quit.'

We never did that up front with quality circles. When teams didn't get what they wanted they kind of got disgruntled and disbanded. Because they weren't as effective in management's mind, we kept skipping from this to this to this to this. I believe that if had we kept quality circles going years ago, I'm talking in the early 80's, I believe that we'd have more true self-managed work teams today. I believe self-managed work teams have to evolve. Especially, in a company that's already established.

You're fighting 'the culture.' You're fighting past history, the way areas are set up. It's very hard to change people. They are very set in their ways and resistant to change. You don't have that with a new company just starting up. When they hire in off the street, guess what? They know they are going to be on a team—they know that is part of the job.

Therefore, it's a little easier to structure it so that they know that part of their job is to meet and solve problems. In our situation, we never forced people to solve problems. On the EQUA, they evolved because somebody, Dave Curry, started these groups and leaders—it wasn't leaders at that time, just key people, started meeting them on a regular basis. It wasn't formally called anything and it evolved on its own."

Employees can be your best problem solvers if you'll give them the rope to run with as did, Dave Barrett. Who else better qualified to understand the problems than the people dealing with them day in and day out? The bottom line benefit to businesses is reduced costs, quicker production, higher productivity, reduced scrap, and higher quality—yielding better value to consumers.

LEARN FROM EMPLOYEES

In researching for a seminar, I interviewed assistant managers at various retail stores. I asked these assistant managers what they didn't like about their manager. Collectively, they gave me an earful. "Quit being a desk manager, get out on the floor," was what I heard most—additionally, they suggested:

Build a Safety net. They would like their managers to hear this message: "Back your assistants." This brings up a critical issue—safety nets. Managers should "grow" their employees in an environment that encourages risk. Train them to make decisions and then support the decisions you've trained them to make. Sure you can reserve the right to suggest they handle the situation differently the next time, but for now BACK THEM! You get the behavior you reward—reward decision making and risk taking.

A manufacturing example comes from Levi Strauss & Co. "I learned that leadership is like raising a kid," says Lynne Southard, a middle manager at Levi. She recalled a situation, which cost the company dearly, one of her people failed to buy enough fabric to meet a production run of jeans. "We sat down and found out what went wrong and how to prevent it in the future in a non-threatening way," explains Southard. "Unlike the old days, there was no blaming and finger pointing."[105]

Stop holding a parking space. "He/she's afraid I'll take their job." Face it, every manager has confronted this issue, an employee being better at certain aspects of the job than the supervisor. It's like getting a great parking space right up front on a busy day—you hate to give it up! Be careful of treating any employee like a parking space and holding on for your exclusive use longer than needed. Promote those who are deserving, even if losing them means additional work for you.

Be a listening leader. All too often I hear, "Listen to me like you truly want to hear what I have to say." Any leader worth his/her salt listens. No! Not just politely paying attention while thinking of something else. My suggestion is that you stop and listen as if your very own life depends on what the person has to say. Actually, your business life (career) does depend on what your employees have to say. They can make you into a star or what the pigeons drop from the sky—the choice is yours.

Walk your talk. The manager who constantly reminds assistants that they should have a life away from the job but constantly change the assistant's schedule appears not to care. I repeatedly heard comments like: "I wish the boss would care about my needs too!" Would you listen to a dentist's lecture about the value of flossing if you, plain as day, could see his or her teeth rotting? How about a 5' 10", 250 pound doctor telling you to loose 20 pounds? Let's face it—you wouldn't heed their warning. Partnering with employees requires integrity from all, especially the boss.

Bringing this thought home—you can't expect your lieutenants to care for, and motivate your troops, if you're not walking your own talk or practicing what you preach. When an owner or manager cares enough to consult with their key staff, candid dialogue becomes possible and true learning can occur. This will bridge to quality relationships, which is the essence of partnering.

Try the *three on three method*. Ask your assistants to share three things they like about the way you manage them. Then simply say, "Thank you" and proceed to ask for three things they *don't* like about the way you manage them. Again, *do not* defend your position, simply say, "Thank you." When you are alone, think about what they had to say. Remember, there's no value in shooting the messenger—especially if the message is accurate!

The only way to build quick rapport with staff is through understanding and utilizing mirroring skills, or large amounts of cash. The latter does not give you long term results. Rather than worry about instant results, work on the kind of quality communication that will deliver lasting improvement. This happens from two-way trust and respect. Back-stabbing should not be tolerated. Statements like: "If you don't like it, there's plenty of other people who want your job" or my favorite idiotic statement, "Don't let the door hit your rear end on the way out!"

Remember, people need a little encouragement once in a while and assistance in believing what they do is valuable. An example of showing employees you care about them is what Tom Springgate does. He's a store manager for a California drug chain, Longs Drug Stores. His store is one of the two anchors located in a strip shopping center. He wanted to increase the value of a sidewalk sale event for his customers, so he invited the local meat market to bring their 20 foot long bar-b-que to fill the air with aroma, and sell sandwiches to customers.

To guarantee the meat markets revenues for the event, he purchased meal tickets for all the employees who worked that day. The whole thing only cost the store only about $100, but the result was Tom showing up as a hero in his employees' eyes. He believes that the breaking of bread with employees has a special ability to bring down the barriers between management and labor. Tom seizes every opportunity to have store meals, pushing communication to a higher level.

MANAGEMENT BY PARTNERING AROUND

Management By Partnering Around (MBPA) is the best possible solution to greater productivity. This applies to anybody who considers themselves a manager or better yet, a leader. Use Ken Blanchard's model from the *One Minute Manager*, find employees doing things right and give them a "one minute praising" on the spot. What a great way to build relationships.

When I suggest partnering around, I'm simply suggesting that you create mini-alliances throughout your organization with employees, teams, executives, and others. Like in networking, your goal in MBPA is to get to know as many people (who work for your company and otherwise) as possible and learn what they're good at—get to know their strengths, weaknesses, and their interests. This knowledge will allow you to successfully put people together using the "Adaptive Organization" model. It will serve you well by unleashing employee creativity and more effectively utilizing their unique abilities.

THE ADAPTIVE ORGANIZATION

This is a strategy currently being used at various levels by such companies as; Becton Dickinson in New Jersey; Apple Computer in Cupertino, California; Cypress Semiconductor in San Jose, California; Levi Strauss in San Francisco, California; Xerox; and AES (formerly Applied Energy Services). This bureaucracy busting practice embraces employee partnering, resulting in better customer service and greater marketplace competitiveness. An informal association exists parallel to, and within, a more formal structured organization. In this process, employees are trained to closely view their work or projects and to devise ways to improve upon them. Frequently, this might mean temporarily leaving one's regular job to join an ad hoc team assaulting a specific challenge of the structured organization.

In 1990, an informal team at Xerox, consisting of people from accounting, sales, distribution and administration, saved the company $200 million in inventory costs. "We're never going to out-discipline the Japanese on quality," explains Paul Allaire, CEO at Xerox. He continues, "To win, we need to find ways to capture the creative and innovative spirit of the American Worker. That's the real organizational challenge."[106]

Incorporating the informal organization, the adaptive organization draws its strength from the energy created by employees realizing openings for utilizing their creativity and initiative. These attributes are usually only characteristics of small, entrepreneurial companies. By aligning with what corporations generally want—innovation and improvement —employees can also get what they want—the opportunity to use their heads and enlarge their skills base.

AES CEO, Roger Sant, invented something called, work week, as part of an effort to encourage everyone from the rank and file, to the executive suite in taking more initiative. One week a year, every senior manager is required to spend a week working in one of the company's generating plants—the employees get to select the executive's assignment.

Work week assisted Sant in denouncing obstacles he identified in the organization. Workers would tell him something couldn't be done because "they" wouldn't go for the idea. Realizing, there was actually no "they,"—only old inefficient habits and memories of past policies—Sant started a "Theybusters" campaign, complete with appropriate buttons and posters. The results were astonishing. One employee figured out how to avoid costly plant shutdowns, by using tennis balls to temporarily stop leaks in a pollution-control system.[107]

THE SCANLON PLAN TODAY

The idea of employee/employer partnering needs to be more than, how much one can get from another. Bringing employees to the level of "ownership level participation" takes involving them in the areas of the business, that affect their lives. You must make them feel as if they truly do matter and have some power over their daily situation. Great employees are one of your most successful marketing strategies.

If you really want to partner with your employees, many possibilities exist. One such model is the Scanlon Plan and it is one of the best kept organizational secrets for successful employee involvement, through equity and responsibility sharing. Two excellent examples, both cited in the book, *The 100 Best Companies to Work for in America*, partly on the basis of their use of the Scanlon Plan are, Donnelly Corporation in Holland, Michigan ($271 million in 1992[108]), and Herman Miller, Inc. located in Zeeland, Michigan ($804 million in 1991/1992[109]).

Father of the plan, Joe Scanlon, was invited to join the faculty at Massachusetts Institute of Technology (MIT) in 1946, because of the foresight of Douglas McGregor (Theory Y/Theory X). At the same time, McGregor invited six young instructors to introduce social science into the engineering curriculum, Carl F. Frost, Ph.D., included. The plan was introduced into several New England organizations, but Joe Scanlon died in 1956, and MIT had limited its interest.

Frost was invited to become a member of the Department of Psychology in 1949, as part of Michigan State University's aggressive postwar effort to meet the needs of the state's change from an agricultural to an industrial based economy.[110]

Frost, recognized by many as today's foremost authority on the Scanlon Plan wrote:

"The most fundamental problem stems from 'ignorance.' American employees, even though better educated, became ignorant of the impact of the international competition for quality. They forgot (if they ever knew) that the only reason they had jobs is because they had customers. They had not been informed, or 'educated,' as to who their customers were. They were not informed about what was required to get a customer—quality, on-time delivery, price—or why they lost a customer. They were not notified as to what competitors or countries were taking their jobs away from them."[111]

Following a presentation by Frost, in the spring of 1950, Herman Miller implemented the Scanlon Plan. Along with responsibility sharing, comes equity sharing—employees receive a monthly bonus based on performance in comparison to the company's business plan. From 1950 to 1984, employees at Herman Miller, received an average yearly bonus of 10.44 percent.[112] Max De Pree, Chairman of the Board at Herman Miller and celebrated author of *Leadership Is An Art* and *Leadership Jazz* (De Pree dedicated this book to Mr. Frost), states, "Participative ownership offers Herman Miller a competitive edge."[113]

Donnelly embraced the Scanlon Plan in the 1950s after a Donnelly driver saw employees receiving their equity sharing checks at Herman Miller and asked, founder, John Donnelly if they could do the same. Asking Dwane Baumgardner, CEO if they would ever consider abandoning the Scanlon Plan, he said:

> "No! We strongly believe that it is critical to the success of any organization. The principles are enduring. We characterize them as the roots of the treaty. We just think they're fundamental. Identity, knowing the right job, where you're going, how you're going to measure doing the job right, participation, equity, competence, all the dimensions."[114]

When asked if the Scanlon Plan could be considered the roots of today's partnering paradigm, Baumgardner said, *"Absolutely!"* Today the Scanlon Plan or *Process*, as it is sometimes referred to, is recognized as a system of total development consisting of assumptions about human behavior, a set of principles for the management of organizations, and a participative process of implementation.

It's said to be a misconception to view the Scanlon Plan narrowly as an incentive system, quality of work life program, suggestion plan, paternalistic employee relations activity, or anti-union strategy. In fact, it is not a plan at all in the sense that it does not specify a mechanistic procedure to be followed in standardized fashion. No two Scanlon Plans are alike. Rather, it is a demanding process to achieve organizational productivity and human self-fulfillment. Through research and experience, four principles have validated the Scanlon Plan and serve as conditions of Scanlon Plan success:

1. **Identity**—the continual process of clarifying and understanding the organization's "mandate," (i.e., requirements to serve customers, owners/shareholders, and employees). This process includes: recognition and affirmation by the majority of employees of the need to change, in order to, manage more effectively all of the organization's resources: marketplace, financial, physical, and human.

2. **Participation**—acceptance by all employees of responsibility for the mandate, and the opportunity to responsibly influence the decision-making process. Participation includes accountability for one's own job and to all who have vested interest in the enterprise.

3. **Equity**—the assurance of a fair and balanced return to customers (product value, quality, delivery, fair price), owners (profitability, return on investment, growth), and employees (job security, competitive wages and benefits, sharing in productivity gains).

4. **Managerial Competence**—the unequivocal requirement of leadership to define the "right job," to be open to influence, and to create a climate for productivity improvements. The identity, participation, and equity processes are demanding tests of managerial attitudes, abilities, and performance.[115]

Adopting a plan like this would be a enormous undertaking, and would be worth the time, energy, and cost if viewed over the long-haul. Unfortunately, too many companies today are more concerned with next quarter's profits than the company's resilience and future. Hopefully, you will examine the possibility of sanctioning the Scanlon Plan at your company.

Baumgardner says, "We're in the state of becoming, the Scanlon process is always in the state of becoming, so we're always working to advance our knowledge on how to better work with each one of the partners in the firm, from the customers all the way through."[116]

Frost asserts, "The prerequisite in each of these companies has been the ability and willingness of executives to lead, rather than to manage. Leadership in the Scanlon Process depends on management's willingness to serve, rather than, be served."[117]

EMPOWER YOUR EMPLOYEES

"Most managers think that if they give away their authority, they are diminished," says Roger Tompkins at State Farm Insurance. "I find exactly the opposite to be the case, but people without internal strength cannot successfully do this." He goes on to say, "I've always tried as a senior guy, to treat everyone up and down the line as an equal, the key to success with people is to treat them as associates rather than a boss/subordinate relationship. In partnering, each helps the other to be successful."[118]

Conventional wisdom traditionally suggested that managers did the thinking, supervisors did the talking, and labor or front line employees did the doing. If you want empowered employees—employees at all levels of thinking, talking, and doing—you want to partner. I believe that partnering is the answer to employee empowerment and empowered employees (ones who think, communicate, and act) are the answer to partnering with your customers. Giving front line employees the authority to handle customer problems does not diminish a manager's power, as Tompkins said, on the contrary—it gives a manager more power—personal power.

To successfully lead employees, one must have this personal power—the kind of power that draws people rather than controls them. This kind of power comes from letting go. Casting off unfounded ideas that more is possible through absolute control. As you allow the powerful inner you to surface, your self esteem will increase. You'll realize that, who you are, is enough and that wearing a facade is not necessary. Most people are bright enough to see through masks and will find it much easier to follow a person of substance over a person without.

Empowerment is so important, because through giving power, a higher level of personal power is possible. Customers want more—more of everything, except price. The logical solution is to enroll your employees in helping. They will only stretch if they feel they can make a difference—if you let them—they will.

"How do I empower my employees?" Change your company culture. I realize this is easier said than done, but isn't it time to make a change in your organization anyway? As you proceed with the steps to partnering, the steps to empowerment will parallel. Take a risk—believe in people and treat them the way they want to be treated. You'll be amazed at the results.

Leona Helmsley might disapprove from her jail cell, but employee empowerment is coming at last to the front desks of the nation's hotels. Starting in 1992, Ritz-Carlton Hotel Co., permitted front-desk clerks to take off up to $2,000 from a guest's bill. (No formal rules had existed previously.)[119]

What about the customer who doesn't speak up for what they want? How do you serve those quiet customers who desire the similar service to what the *squeaky wheel* gets, but doesn't have the nerve to ask? I challenged Tom Benson of Mitsubishi with this question:

"Two dimensions to that. The word *empowerment* is becoming a big word these days. You have to have an organization that is empowered to make those type of decisions that when somebody is not smart enough to sit down and call me here, but is smart enough to go to the service manager or the service adviser in a dealership and express themselves, those same people have to be empowered to make those kind of decisions that I would make up here [at headquarters].

Anyone who comes in contact with the customer has to be trained to handle the customers' problems. You have to have an organization that is empowered to establish the partnership. This is the direction we're going, but it is not something that you can just say. If you don't have the systems and processes to empower you, you're not empowered, even though I tell you you're empowered.

That's the first step—you have to make sure that the people know they're empowered, and that the systems and the processes are there to support that empowerment. It's not easy to do because it means you have to give up some control—number one—and you've got to get the people to accept that control. This is harder to do than the first step. A lot of people would rather just say, 'Tell me what to do and I'll do it. Don't put me in a position where I have to make the tough decisions all the time.'"

In questioning employee accountability, Tom responded, "Responsibility not accountability. Accountability is kind of negative. We want them to accept the responsibility. So that's the first thing we do. The second thing you have to do is, to transmit that all back to the customer so the customer knows you're wanting to serve them. The customers today, don't always realize that you really want to take care of them and want them to be happy with what they buy. That's where our customer surveys come in. We call them and say, 'Are you happy with your car and if you're not, what are you unhappy about?' Then that information is given to the people who can take some action. You simply can't stop there, you have to continue to do this periodically throughout the life of the vehicle. That's what we're putting into force."[120]

We have all listened to stories of exemplary service from an employee, maybe even experienced the wonderful results from an empowered employee. But, have you listened with an ear for action? Have you said, "That's great for their business but it would never work in mine!" How do you know if you never gave it a try? If you truly empower your employees—pat yourself on the back and say to yourself, "Good Job!" If not, you must understand your employees are the key to your success in partnering with your customers—don't you think it's time you give them a chance? Bill Eaton, a member of the Levi Strauss executive management committee does. Eaton attests, "On a day-to-day basis, my passion comes from backing people's efforts, getting them what they need to do the job, educating them, and working with them as a member of the team."[121]

In the days when I would hire and train sales persons for a consumer products importer, I would tell my apprentices, "Do it my way until you become successful. Then, when you discover an even better way to get our products into retail stores, let me know and we'll all do it your way!"

I asked Dwane Baumgardner what the greatest thing he as a CEO could personally do to partner with his employees. His assertion, "Try to be visible to them—I don't do enough of that. Be articulate regarding where we're going with the company and we're constantly reinforcing our values."[122]

In 1991, Steelcase's Context plant was named by *Industry Week,* along with nine others in various industries, as America's Best. The ten were chosen on the basis of quantifiable results, overall competitiveness, and emphasis on employee empowerment.[123] Employees at the plant work in teams and have implemented several money-saving ideas. The total savings in a little more than a year after starting production have amounted to $1.2 million. In fact, one employee in the distribution department came up with an idea that is now saving Steelcase $150,000 a year.

Visiting the plant, I was impressed with the level of enthusiasm among both the management, and workers alike. They all enjoyed an environment of collaboration.

TIPS FOR PARTNERING WITH EMPLOYEES

1. Listen to them and act on what they say. It's quite discouraging to offer a suggestion when asked, and they are not used. You can pull it off a couple times, but after that, you'll get nothing from employees.

2. Encourage them to share ideas on how you could help them balance their lives, but don't put your nose where it's not wanted.

3. Give them daily freedom. Allow them to occasionally adjust their hours to accommodate family needs.

4. Be flexible with work shifts. Some may prefer four 10 hour days to five 8 hour. Let me caution you about the legality of the "alternative work week" idea—many states have regulations that are more restrictive than those of the federal government. While your state may be more relaxed in the issue, I recommend you contact your labor commissioner.

    California is the most restrictive of all states in regulations. Requiring employers to draft a formal written disclosure as to the rules and what effects the policy will have on their employees. Employers are also required to hold a meeting of employees, answering questions about the plan fully. Then, a secret ballot must be held, requiring two-thirds majority of employees to be approved. Manufacturers in California must also submit a copy of their plan to the State Labor Commissioner. An additional suggestion, keep a copy of the plan forever, even if you later abandon the plan—to protect you from possible fines.

135

Another caution is that, it is illegal, to deduct from an employee's paycheck in a prejudgment action. Like deducting the cost of an item they may have broken if the employee refuses to pay (U.S. Supreme Court decision, Sniadach vs. Family Finance, 1969).

5. Offer both sexes the same options in handling personal situations.

6. Set goals and timetables for every project—make sure everybody is clear on your expectations from the start.

7. Don't be an absentee manager and expect everything to be done your way—you're not there so how could you know what's needed?

8. Accept the responsibility—if something didn't work out right. I'm sure if you look close, you have some accountability for the end results. Remember you trained them.

9. Show them their job is important, no matter what it might be by offering to assist them in times of need. Maybe even offer to take over a less desirable activity in busy or frantic times. Letting your employees see you do the dirty work once in a while builds moral.

10. Don't talk marriage but act like it's a one-night stand.

"If a man is called to be a streetsweeper, he should sweep streets even as Michelangelo painted, or Beethoven composed music, or Shakespeare wrote poetry. He should sweep streets so well that all the hosts of heaven and earth will pause to say, here lived a great streetsweeper who did his job well."

-Martin Luther King, Jr.

SEVEN

BECOMING THE OPTIMAL PARTNER

You the business owner, executive, and/or the company, complete the partnering pentad star. Though I stated before that the pentad does not revolve around you, the pentad is not possible without you. You must provide the leadership, vision, and enthusiasm to make the pentad work. It simply won't work without you.

At Mitsubishi Motor Sales, the executive team really understands that it's up to them to lead the charge, that being the optimal partner is critical to partnering success. They know that without the executive suite beating the partnering drum, very little happens. It wasn't always that way. Most of the executive team came from the American automotive industry and they thought they were going to build a different kind of company. Dan McNamara, senior vice president of corporate administration at Mitsubishi Motor Sales related their story.[124] In the late 1980s, seven or eight years into it, as the organization was maturing, the executives looked around and realized they hadn't developed a partnering situation. They had built the antithesis of what they had planned—company politics and back stabbing—they had a sickness within.

Lucky enough, they realized they had a problem. The company was young and the culture flexible—they believed change was possible. After several flawed attempts to change, using popular management quick fixes and learning buzzwords, Richard (Dick) Recchia, executive vice president, general operations and COO, went off for an afternoon to develop a new mission statement. The statement was published, distributed, and not followed. They then realized that gimmicks were not going to work.

Later, they started to talk about values and realizing, with the assistance of outside consultants, that people's behavior is grounded in their underlying values. This led them to a model for ranking values, both individual, and collectively. They found that the key was to identify those values and align those values with the kind of company they wanted to be. As the management team started understanding their own individual values, they were surprised at how similar their values were collectively. The executives realized that they each were not alone in putting high value on family and personal life.

From this foundation, they stared a visioning process—Recchia went off to a hotel room, with a consultant, to articulate his vision for the company on paper. Next, the executive team went on a two and one-half day retreat, focusing on only three issues:

- Breaking down the barriers that existed.
- Recchia sharing his vision.
- Recchia inviting the team to expand his vision, encompassing their additional values.

The result of the retreat was an expanded vision for the company—not one that Recchia had to "sell" to his executive team, but one expanded by the team, in which they had ownership. The next step was to share this vision with the next level of management, about 30 people. Again, getting this level of management's personal ownership in the vision through their additional input. Then appointed these 30 plus managers to carry the vision throughout the company.

McNamara recalled, "We made a mistake!" As the managers were carrying the message throughout the ranks, the executive team, rather than pushing ahead and further working in the new vision, moved on to other challenges and assumed their managers could make the cultural change alone. The change they wanted wasn't possible because the employees did not experience the executives changing their behavior and pushing for the new culture. McNamara told me they lost about a year.

Learning from their misfortunes, the executive team started again with the process, taking charge and showing the employees by example that they meant, and would live by what they professed. Following this enlightened genesis, the executives set out to change departmental policies that were not in alignment with the vision. As an example, human resources had been reviewing employees, giving them a numerical grade, like in school. Eventually, the review process was changed to a "Values Initiate Performance" (VIP), where numbers were replaced by a values based system that was "individual driven," focusing on their growth and not holding them accountable for a corporate "guesstimate."

The value Mitsubishi has received as a result of their change:

- Communications improvement. Reduced politics, back-stabbing, and hidden agendas, along with, an increased willingness by employees to partner interdepartmentally, keeping others informed.
- Greater productivity through increased creativity and risk taking.

The Mitsubishi executive team believed that they could build a better company, one in which partnering was part of their culture. Once they were clear on their vision and allowed it to be expanded by others, things happened. They didn't sell the vision but, allowed others to have ownership by expanding and adding to the primary vision.

After many false starts, the executives became optimal partners by not charging others with executing the company's vision, but by leading the charge and living what they professed. The lessons Mitsubishi learned are universal truths that any business owner, executive, or executive team must embrace to complete their partnering pentad.

NOBODY'S BIGGER THAN THE SYSTEM

In any organization there is a certain need for harmony. What some might consider harmony, others would call anarchy. In being an optimal partner, you must consider the good of the collective company welfare above that of an individual for culture consistency which is necessary for keeping harmony in your company. People need to know what to expect in various situations. In realizing that the good of the whole, takes precedence over an individual's desire, A.W. Tompkins, Sr., Chief Agency Officer at State Farm Insurance from 1930 to 1966, lived by the edict he coined: "Nobody's bigger than the system."

From the 1930s when he first uttered these words, continuing through to the present, this has been a guiding light in State Farm's culture. "You must have an internally consistent view to be an effective executive," advocates Roger Tompkins of State Farm (son of A.W. Tompkins, Sr.). Recalling a time when he was an Agency Vice President and his charge was to increase minority and women agents, he received a call from the home office requesting him to appoint a board director's son as an agent. He stood to his principles and made it clear that the man would have to come to California and join the pool along with the other prospective agents to determine his suitability.

Not long after this, Roger Tompkins was approached by his top agent in Southern California with a similar request for his son. In between a rock and a hard spot, Tompkins, putting this singular relationship at risk, explained to his top agent that the son would have to enter the pool as would any other. This agent wanted to preempt the system. Since ego was at risk, and Tompkins would not bend, the agent felt betrayed and the relationship was destroyed. Tompkins, believing that nobody was bigger than the system took the more difficult path to preserve the trust of the other agents and the integrity of the system.

"This integrity is the fabric of the relationship—the foundation of the marketing partnership between State Farm and their agents," said Tompkins.[125]

Similar and just as insidious, is the code of silence myth, which stems from school days. This has been the root cause in dismantling relationships at a greater frequency than you can imagine. In school, telling on others, or "finking," as it was called when I attended grade school and later referred to as "narcing," in high school (complements of the drug culture), was considered a capitol offence by peers. What a joke! If there truly was a relationship, the one that was wrongly accused of an indiscretion would not have to unjustly face the penalty because, the guilty party would, in respect for the other and not being a taker, come forward and admit guilt—not wanting their innocent friend to suffer. Why I call this code of silence a myth is because, rarely in these situations was there a relationship that was based on integrity. I understand the business environment is different than that of a school, but the principle of integrity remains constant.

How deeply do people trust you, and you, others? Trust has been a core issue woven throughout the pages of this book—trust appears to me, to be the most important ingredient of quality partnering relationships. Stephen Covey, in his book, *The 7 Habits of Highly Effective People*, wrote:

> "To try to change outward attitudes and behaviors does very little good in the long run if we fail to examine the basic paradigms from which those attitudes and behaviors flow."

If you and/or your company have trust issues, I find it hard to believe that you'll succeed in partnering until those issues are resolved. Do you operate from a place of giving or taking? Attending a seminar, a few years back, I was on the receiving end of an exercise where a number of people I respected, offered me feedback as to how they experienced me within the parameters of being a giver or taker. Most, experienced me as a taker—this exercise, simple as it was, had a profound effect on my life and how I have since viewed the world and the choices I've made since. I now believe, that it's impossible to out give the universe, though I try. While I'm not suggesting that you give away your business, I am suggesting that you challenge yourself to view your world through the eyes of integrity. In partnering, you get from giving.

PROFIT FROM BEING THE OPTIMAL PARTNER

At Levi Strauss, they're living what they say. This privately held San Francisco-based company, with 1992 revenues of $5.6 billion is letting action speak louder than words.[126] They're reshaping their corporate culture through dismantling parts of their hierarchy and overhauling how they design, manufacturer, and market their clothing. Chief executive, Robert Haas, a former Peace Corps volunteer and great-great-grandnephew of founder Levi Strauss is being an optimal partner by building ethics into the company's bottom line through ethical practices, empowerment, and an appreciation of diversity. He embraces empowerment, the practice of putting more power into the hands of Levi's employees at all levels and encourages them to become actively involved in corporate decision making.

Levi Strauss is embracing the belief and practice of partnering throughout their many areas of business. Haas suggests that their emphasis on values is "not just nice behavior" but that it is also smart business. He states, "Consumers are looking more and more to the company behind the product. Companies have to wake up to the fact that they are more than a product on a shelf. They're behavior as well."[127] This had much to do with their decision of partial withdrawal from China, citing "pervasive violations of basic human rights" as the reason.

Haas believes that this adherence to business ethics has not hurt the company. In fact he believes the reverse, it has helped the company's profits.

> He contends, "It's clear that our culture is moving, and there's definitely a connection to the financial side. We're on our fifth year of record earnings, and this is in the middle of a bad U.S. economy and sickly economies in Europe."[128]

Haas walks his talk in being an optimal partner by embracing ethical business practices at Levi. He empowers his employees by giving power, rather than by protecting the power with the armor of his position. Similarly, Miles Gordon, CEO at FNIC, advocates that being the optimal partner is their only strategy. In asking Gordon if he believes the ability to adopt partnering is in-bred, he answered:

> "I believe you're not born with it, but it starts from early life. I think it's your family values which, looking back at our company, the people that have really bought into this (which is a lot of people) and especially people that have been around a long time and have orchestrated, family values are very similar. Strong family values, a strong belief in keeping the overhead down, working and not just living off other people. In other words, you earn what you get."[129]

Being an optimal partner is the right thing to do, not just because its ethical, which should be reason enough, but because it pays off, as illustrated by the examples of Levi Strauss & Company, and the numerous others presented throughout this book.

THINKING YOUR WAY THERE

Thinking your way to being an optimal partner is a start. For decades, the late, Dr. Norman Vincent Peal lectured on the possibilities that are available through the power of positive thinking. In his classic *The Power of Positive Thinking*, Peal stated:

"A sense of inadequacy interferes with the attainment of your hopes, but self-confidence leads to self-realization and achievement."

Create for yourself the attitude of limitless partnering possibilities. It's no secret that attitude can and will make the difference between partnering failure and success. Success is what you ultimately want isn't it? It's easier than you think to get into the mind set of "I don't care" or the "I can't do it." It's your self-confidence that will allow you to become the optimal partner—the pentad will not be complete without you!

"In Theory X terms," states Roger Tompkins, "Managers see people as essentially lazy, somewhat stupid, needing constant direction and prodding to get any work done. Theory Y managers, on the other hand, see people as essentially interested in being productive, ready to work, and to cooperate, (if shown the way and given the tools) and essentially self-starting.

As I think about how I have interacted with other associates of the State Farm Insurance Companies, both employees and agents, over the years, I realize I have viewed them through the Theory Y lens. As a result, our 'Marketing Partnership' concept and philosophy, which is so integral to the way we approach serving our customers in the marketplace, has always squared with my personal view of people."[130]

When you get caught in the drift of life and/or business, and you will, it's your partners who will be there for you with strength, energy and enthusiasm to assist you in seeing new and unique solutions to your challenges. This is something on which you could never put a monetary value or price. What you can do is be an optimal partner and reciprocate when your partners, the others in your pentad, are in need. Your partnering alliances have a vested interest in your success, as you do in theirs.

To view your daily concerns, better yet—challenges, from a new perspective, requires that you shift your paradigms. Like the people living in the time of Columbus and Copernicus, you too must challenge your paradigms and shift away from what is not serving you.

Look at it this way: when you look at a tall tree from 50 feet away through a standard 50mm camera lens you see a particular view, not all of the tree. Now change to a macro closeup lens and you see not much of anything. Now change to a wide angle lens and you see just about all of it. What was different each time? The lens, your filter—each of us filters how the world truly is and that's our reality. So, change your filter, your vision, and behold all the new possibilities.

To stretch your partnering muscles, try taking on a lens that a well focused question provides. Ask yourself daily: "Would you enter into a partnering alliance with somebody like you?" If asked habitually, this question will help you to keep activities and decisions in the perspective of being the optimal partner. Ask daily: "Who do I now trust that may serve and be served as my partner?" A sign you might consider posting where it is quite visible: "Who's My Partner Today?"

IT TAKES YOU

Partnering is not for every business and organization, because it takes you having the capability of being an optimal partner to know if partnering is right for your business. Reasons not to partner may include: You may simply view the world from a place of loss and negativity. You have the market cornered (but for how long), and enjoy the power position of calling all the shots. You may be a loner and prefer to go it alone. Maybe you're even satisfied to make do with less. You may not desire to build a partnering pentad—but let me warn you—you can't be in business today without partnering to some degree. Maybe it's partnering with your customers, maybe another area, but you simply cannot operate in a vacuum and survive. If you find yourself having the above negative conversations, find the strength to escape your perceived dungeons. Roger Choquette at Steelcase shares his thoughts.

> "Why don't other companies do this [adopt partnering]? I belong to a partnership roundtable and we, with a number of other manufacturers, talk about distribution because we're all in the management of distribution and it is interesting to me to see the different viewpoints on distribution that exist in major corporations around the country. You have Steelcase who is very much into partnering, very paternalistic, very protective, and invests heavily. This whole department exists strictly for our dealers—our whole job is to grow dealer profitability—that's all we're here for.
> Because financially, a healthy and very strong dealership will ultimately have payback for Steelcase. So you've got Steelcase at one end of the spectrum and then you've got companies at the other end—where distribution is a necessary evil because they don't have a direct sales force. You can hear the comments. You can sense that management has never talked to anybody that distributes their product. Many have never talked to the owners of these companies—they don't invite them in. They don't try and partner with them and then they wonder why they have difficulty in the representation of their line. They wonder why they have competitive products within their distribution channel. You have those two extremes.
> The question I always wonder about is, if partnering works, and I see it working here, then why don't other companies do it? I always labor with the answer. Is it that people don't want to take the time? Don't want to invest the money? They don't see the payoff? I don't know what the answer is."[131]

Operating from a positive foundation of business strategies will give you strength. Find the benefit for your company in you being an optimal partner and begin to build your pentad. This book has repeatedly shown you the benefits and payoffs in partnering. Like Roger Choquette says, "Why don't other companies do this?"

PLATINUM PARTNERING

Maybe you've heard it called the Platinum Rule, or The Golden Rule Expanded—whichever, the concept is, to do unto others the way *they* would have *you* do unto them. To be the optimal partner and company you must see things as your partnering alliance members do, otherwise you'll greatly diminish your possibilities. Think back to great leaders you've had the opportunity with which to interact—haven't they made you comfortable around them? Sure they may have pushed you to achieve more, but that wouldn't have been possible, had they not initially built rapport. They somehow have had the ability to get you to want to perform to your highest level of potential. The same is important for you if you want people and organizations to partner with you.

Learn the skills to understand people, learn how to effectively communicate on their terms rather than yours. Anthony Robbins' book, *Unlimited Power*, is essentially about creating more power within—allowing one to more effectively influence others through effective communications. Robbins says:

> "To me, success is the ongoing process of striving to become more. It is the opportunity to continually grow emotionally, socially, spiritually, physiologically, intellectually, and financially while contributing in some positive way to others. The road to success [or partnering] is always under construction. It is a progressive course, not an end to be reached."

> Dan McNamara at Mitsubishi asserts, "Be sure you're prepared to live the values you profess—your people will 'hear' what they 'see,' not what you say."[132]

In the Korean business culture the principle of *Nunchi*, the ability to look in someone's eyes and understand, allows for a powerful nonverbal communication. Through this process, employees make decisions that reflect how their manager would expect them to decide.[133]   Nunchi also exists as a societal binder and is the reason given by some for Koreans' less outgoing nature as compared to Westerners.   As partnering relationships blossom, this further sense of deeper understanding and communication, becomes more real and less theoretical—assisting in alliance harmony.   Study nunchi, if you can develop the sense, you will become the type of person to which others will gravitate.

FLEXING ONLY THROUGH THE EXECUTIVE SUITE

I was asked by a manager, "How do you flex in changing times, when the culture of the company is not as flexible as the changing times?"   While I believe that much of the book has addressed this concern, the key is in the executive suite.   When the top people in the organization are rigid and unbending—the company culture will follow and flexing is near impossible.   Those sharing the executive suite, must be convinced of two elements before an organization can flex.   First that they will not loose control, (they will) and second, the change will benefit the bottom line.

The issue of control must be approached from the angle of power. As discussed earlier, personal power rather than positional power is what encourages partnering with employees.   The increased bottom line becomes possible when people are empowered to use all that they know, opening the flood gate of creativity and innovation.

There is one suggestion I'd like to offer that I believe can be successful in allowing an organization to flex, bend, and stretch—phasing.   Within the parameters of a schedule, the phasing in of partnering ideas, beliefs, and practices will allow even the most rigid executive to slowly experience the benefits.   This method allows logical progression, flex-points for reassessing strategies, goals, and conditions for change and improvement.

In the final analysis and like with Mitsubishi, flexibility, comes through partnering, but is unlikely unless the executives of a given company embrace the vision.

PERSONAL ACHIEVEMENT IS OKAY

In your effort to become an optimal partner, take accountability for your decisions and actions. The following are some tips to assist you in the direction of ultimate effectiveness. It will become easier for you to be an optimal partner as you put your own house in order. This is because you'll have more time to cultivate the partnering relationships you seek. Take time to not just read, but to study and commit to action on the following:

1. Be aware of your time wasters.
2. Know when you are most productive and do only important activities then.
3. Set priorities rather than just have a "to do" list. High priorities go on top of the list and must be handled before the "fun stuff."
4. Time charts or records will assist you in better knowing where you need work.
5. Get a laptop or notebook computer! It will assist you in managing your time more effectively.
6. Procrastination is your friend-maybe when you retire. Until then, tattoo "DO IT NOW" on the back of your hand.
7. Make every day significant. At the end of each day write one thing in your calendar you did that day that you felt was significant. Do this on a regular basis and you'll access additional inner strength to deal with what you perceive as those really lousy days.

Derailment among business executives is a common occurrence, but it doesn't have to be your paradigm. When you are committed, passion becomes second nature. It's the natural by-product of your commitment. Partner with *yourself* to become an optimal partner.

OPTIMAL PARTNER'S PUBLICITY

Personal publicity will assist you in becoming more secure. The more secure you are the more willing you will become to:

- Take partnering risks.
- Give power to your employees thereby initiating partnering.
- Have trust in others, by realizing you have something valuable to offer your business community or industry.

High profile executives and managers are often sought by companies to become integral parts of their company's organization. The economy is dynamic, ever changing and businesses can no longer afford to keep on the deadwood. Make a commitment to yourself here and now to be a person of substantive and perceived value, continually striving to be more.

As companies go through excruciating reengineering and downsizing, they're looking to their stars for vision and to keep the business alive and healthy. People become stars by publicizing their accomplishments and heroic efforts throughout their company and industry. You too, can do this and it does not preclude you from being a team player and partner. Yes, I understand that it's not your way—the problem is that "your way" may create a one-way ticket to oblivion. Many people need someone to give them permission to do something that their parents once told them was not "our way." I hereby give you permission to promote yourself to the world!

As a colleague, Mark Victor Hanson, has told me many times, "Let your inner knower tell you what to do." Your inner knower can assist you to see your true value to the economy in which you participate. Let go of your "stuff" and move on to your potential!

Three reasons why professionals and executives are hesitant to promote themselves:

1. Feel it's too self-important, pompous, pontifical, pretentious, stuffy, grandiose, ostentatious or stuffy.
2. Not in keeping with the professional image they desire to

project.

3.   Believe promotion costs more than the value they receive.

The only restraint that keeps you from having the public image and stature that many enjoy is the conversation you have with yourself about the additional possibilities for your life. Dislodge those old head tapes that have been immobilizing your personal and partnering efforts to get ahead. Launch them right out of your consciousness.

YOU CAN MAKE THE DIFFERENCE

As a platform speaker, trainer, and consultant, I consider myself successful when assisting others to shift and see new potentiality. In fact, my stand in life is *Empowering people to see and choose new possibilities for their lives.* Recently, one of my students, Craig Swarens, a manufacturing manager who supervises about a hundred employees submitted an enlightened paper:

"I read *They Shoot Managers Don't They* [by Dr. Terry Paulson] in February during a Boy Scout snow trip. It was very interesting and had terrific ideas on making improvements. Full of this knowledge and inspired, I rushed into work Monday morning, brought some people into my office and explained my idea to change a procedure affecting both the stock room and the production floor. Since I was the boss, it was agreed upon and put into effect.

This one small change saved many labor hours since then and will in the future but the program stopped there. I was happy for a few days that this had worked and slowly forgot what I had read, the inspiration faded and no other improvements were made. The information was there, the opportunity was there, but the reinforcement and commitment was not enough to keep me going.

My first note from Terry's lecture was 'change never stops'—well it did for me two weeks after reading the book. Maybe we should say "change shouldn't ever stop" if perfection or improvement is the goal. I can say that since reading the book I

151

have been more open to suggested changes from both within and without my departments. I had been getting more and more set in my ways in the last few years and have found myself saying things like, "We've always done it that way—why change now?" So a more open mind on my part is a big change for the better!"

The "Dimmer Switch Syndrome" is usually a paralyzer of improvement. As it was explained to me by Artie Maren: Visualize yourself in a room with completely sealed doors and windows—eliminating all outside influences. You have materials to keep yourself happily occupied but you're without a clock. The lights are controlled by a computerized rheostat (dimmer switch) of which you have absolutely no control. Over a period of a month you contently live your life, sleeping when you wish, eating when you wish and doing what you wish. The computer is dimming the lights so slowly that you cannot perceive a change. At the end of the month you are pleasantly unaware that you are living in almost total darkness—and it seems normal.

This is what happens to most people in one way or another, be it their family, relationship, health or career. One day you wake up seeing yourself as a different person than you had prior. This is what I think Craig Swarens was referring to. While I'm not sure perfection as he suggested is possible, he was on the money when suggesting that improvement shouldn't ever stop. Partnering, without a doubt is an improvement enabler and improvement ultimately translates into greater profits. Becoming an optimal partner takes casting off life-long and closely-held myths.

"While No-Limit people are generally perceived to be functioning at higher levels in their lives, it is important here to describe the thinking qualities which separate them from other individuals, without making it sound as though everyone who is not a No-Limit person is somehow inferior or neurotic. People who display No-Limit characteristics seem to look at the world differently. They see everything in the world as an opportunity, rather than as something to be feared or avoided.

No-Limit people think from a perspective of mastery rather than coping in their lives. That is, they feel that they are determiners of their own fate, rather than always adjusting to life's circumstances."

-Wayne Dyer[134]

John Murphy, director of purchasing for Teledyne-Laars in Moorpark, California, a sizable company that makes pool and spa heaters, stretched beyond his comfort zone in an effort to be a no-limit individual by writing the following poem about partnering. I feel it captures the essence of partnering.

Partnering is so fine
just like a rare red wine
It can save a company from the Grime
by decreasing its "cycle time."

Partnering is for fun
and it's only just begun.
So if your company is on the run
it's time to get yourself at least one.

Partnering is where it's at
it will make your structure flat.
Not to mention your profits fat,
and your customers sit and chat.

Partnering is for all the changes to be made
from high finance to local trade.
It's for the plans that you've laid
and for all the roads yet to pave.

Partnering is for the knowing
and it'll keep the cash flowing.
It will aid great growing
and your wonderful wisdom showing.

So for those of you who cannot see
and for those who don't agree.
If the decision were left to me,
I'd look twice, for **Partnering is to be!**

The confidence it took for this self-professed, ex-bean counter to stretch and write a poem was monumental. If Murphy can do it so can you—partner that is—not write a poem. Truly, it will take plenty of confidence to partner at the level I'm suggesting, yet the prize easily out-weighs the risk. Be confident in your decision to adopt the partnering paradigm for your company. Create the synergy that you know is possible through partnering.

TIPS FOR HOW TO FAIL AT PARTNERING

This list was adapted from a humorous, but unpublished paper submitted in one of my classes, titled: *A Manual For Partnering—How to Fail at Partnering Without Really Trying*, by Darlene Voosen.

- Maintain a competitive attitude rather than a cooperative attitude.
- Don't trust your partner any—by all means keep secrets from them.
- Belittle your employees. Treat them as if they were the mindless robots.
- Offer no support from upper management. Make partnering, the force of the month.
- Maintain full control—you cannot trust your partner—don't let

them have any information about your product or service.

- Communication should be kept at a minimum. Partners should not share ideas for getting things accomplished or concerns about possible problems.
- Do not be flexible and insist that your partners do business your way. Be resistant to suggestions from your partner for improvement. Insist that this is the way you do business—they can either take it or leave it!
- As for your employees, one manager expresses his viewpoint: "You were not hired to think!"
- Don't give your employees any control or empowerment. Don't give them the authority to stop the assembly line if the product is substandard.
- Suggestion boxes may be put up but don't incorporate any of the suggestions.
- Don't give your employees any recognition or rewards. After all they get a paycheck each week.
- Each month try some different improvement process. If it doesn't work move on to something else—latest "flavor of the month." Employees and partners will actually look forward to next month.

A FINAL WORD

Copernicus did away with the belief of a fixed earth, situated at the hub of the Aristotelian-Ptolemaic universe. In his cosmos the earth revolved around the central sun in an annual orbit and at the same time executed its daily rotations. You too can make a difference by casting off antiquated business beliefs and embracing the ultimate business strategy, partnering. Build, honor, and respect the many entities, people and relationships of your Copernican Pentad.

Partnering will not solve all your business challenges, in fact partnering will create some now ones. By adopting the partnering paradigm, you will have access through relationships, to more possibilities for your business than you would have considered possible. Ever since I can remember, speakers at seminars I've attended and colleagues, have told me that the power is less in the knowing and more in the doing that makes people successful. What do you plan to do about what you've learned from this book? This book you now hold in your hand will be a valuable tool—but only if you go into action. Adopt the ideas and lessons, use this book as your partnering resource. "Set your sights high, but don't be disappointed when you don't attain all your objectives," recommends Dave Elliott at Technicolor. "Always shoot high."

In aiming, don't wait for all your "partnering ducks" to be in a row before you start. If you do, this will simply be just another book you read and said, "Sounds good, hope I can use it some day." You've now invested too much of your valuable time to just blow it off. Your power comes from action. We both know what can happen—you'll put the book on the shelf with all the others that proceeded it or you might give this book to a friend in an effort to "fix them" and the window of opportunity simply fades into the sunset. Another great concept, of which no advantage will be taken. Take action today—achieve success in your life.

> "Remember this: Every man who accomplishes anything worthwhile in his life will leave behind him many temples still unfinished when he departs this life." G.J. Mecherle, founder, State Farm Insurance Companies.

I respectfully submit to that you look closely at your goals and priorities in life and, as did Ebenezer Scrooge, in *A Christmas Carol*, heighten your priority on relationships, thereby making room in your business universe for partnering and the partnering pentad.

The outer star is complete. All that's left is to add the shaded pentagon in the center. The center represents what I call the art of partnering—the relationships, rudiments, principles, and components of the pentad that hold together, connect, and support the formidable bond necessary for your pentad to prosper. In maintaining your partnering pentad, the key to partnering success is relationships. Protect them as you would your only child.

I've endeavored not only to bring you to the source, but more importantly to make you thirsty for the possibilities that partnering can bring to your business. The choice to make partnering a part of your business culture is yours. Dwane Baumgardner, CEO at Donnelly believes that partnering is the strategy for long-term success. He states:

> "It's deeply ingrained in our culture, it's woven into the fabric." Asking him how long the partnering belief has permeated Donnelly's halls, he replied, "Decades. As long as we can remember. I've been here for almost 25 years."[135]

> Miles Gordon of FNIC articulates, "A concept I grew up with since I was a child is, make enough money for everybody and everybody can win."[136]

Money and success are definitely reasons for partnering—possibly the most propelling. Financial security, which is possible and likely through partnering, is necessary to provide the means to live your life in this modern world. But, what about success? Is success measured by money? Might success be measured by the total sum of the parts—meaning whom and what you have chosen to become?

For me, success is the *Peak of Satisfaction* I receive when a journey is completed or a challenge is overcome. When I achieve what I set out to do, have results in my life, I am successful. Success is a feeling rather than a tangible position in life. What is success for you? Can others, through partnering, be a part of your success? For challenging conventional wisdom, Copernicus received a 500 year excommunication. What price are you willing to pay for progress?

NOTES

1. Interview, December 14, 1992

2. Telephone interview, April 28, 1993

3. *Los Angeles Times*, May 19, 1992

4. *Financial World*, September 29, 1992

5. Interview, December 31, 1992

6. *Fortune*, April 8, 1991

7. Interview, December 14, 1992

8. Letter from Roger Tompkins, January 8, 1993

9. Interview, November 17, 1992

10. Ibid

11. Interview, December 17, 1992

12. *Engineering News-Record*, October 14, 1991

13. Interview, December 14, 1992

14. *Industry Week*, January 7, 1991

15. Interview, November 16, 1992

16. Interview, November 19, 1992

17. Interview, November 20, 1992

18. Interview, November 18, 1992

19. Interview, November 16, 1992

20. Interview, February 22, 1993

21. Interview, November 17, 1992

22. Letter from Roger Tompkins, January 8, 1993

23. Terry L. Paulson, Ph.D., *They Shoot Managers Don't They*, (Berkeley: Ten Speed, 1991)

24. Lee Iacocca, *Iacocca—An Autobiography*, (New York: Bantam Books, 1984)

25. Gene Slowinski, Ph.D., Organizational Dynamics, (Gladstone, New Jersey)

26. Interview, November 18, 1992

27. Jack Farmer, Jr., DuPont construction manager, DeLisle, Louisiana. *Engineering News-Record*, October 14, 1991

28. T. Michael Goodrich, BE&K Inc., Birmingham, Alabama. *Engineering News-Record*, October 14, 1991

29. Interview, November 17, 1992

30. Interview, November 11, 1992

31. Interview, November 18, 1992

32. Letter from Roger Tompkins, January 8, 1993

33. Interview, November 16, 1992

34. Interview, November 18, 1992

35. Interview, November 16, 1992

36. Interview, November 11, 1992

37. Don Woutat, "GM-Energy Department Research to be Denied to Japanese," *Los Angeles Times*, January 24, 1992

38. Caleb Solomon, "What Really Pollutes? Study of a Refinery Provides an Eye-Opener," *The Wall Street Journal*, March 29, 1993

39.Patrick Lee, "Chrysler Gets an Electric Car Partner," *Los Angeles Times*, March 4, 1992

40. Jonathan Weber, "In Search of Computing's Holy Grail," *Los Angeles Times*, September 27, 1992

41. Ronald C. Williams, Partnering Program Manager for Arizona Department of Transportation

42. Telephone interview, January 1993

43. Dean Witter/NationsBank news release, October 26, 1992

44. *Through the Years...Philosophies*, (State Farm Insurance Companies: Bloomington, Illinois)

45. Interview, November 20, 1992

46. Interview, November 16, 1992

47. John Scully, *Odyssey—Pepsi to Apple...*, (Harper & Row: New York, 1987)

48. Interview with Maryam Komejan, Donnelly Corporation, Corporate Secretary, November 18, 1992

49. Michael J. McCarthy, *The Wall Street Journal*, October 1, 1991

50. Dave Szymamski, *The Tampa Tribune*, February 17, 1992

51. Damon Darlin, *The Wall Street Journal*, October 1, 1991

52. Chris Woodyard, *Los Angeles Times*, January 6, 1993

53. Leslie Helm, *Los Angeles Times*, July 6, 1992

54. John Lippman, "Selling of a Disney Celebration," *Los Angeles Times*, October 2, 1991

55. Teresa Watanabe, *Los Angeles Times*, November 24, 1992

56. *The Wall Street Journal*, March 23, 1993

57. G. Pascal and Bob Ortega, *The Wall Street Journal*, March 10, 1993

58. Interview, July 1991

59. Interview, November 18, 1992

60. Ibid

61. James Flanigan, *Los Angeles Times*, September 20, 1992

62. *Success Selling*, May 1993

63. *The Wall Street Journal*, March 31, 1993

64. *The Wall Street Journal*, March 17, 1993

65. James S. Hirsh, *The Wall Street Journal*, March 11, 1993

66. Robert B. Tucker, *Managing the Future*, (New York: G.P. Putnam's Sons, 1991)

67. *The Wall Street Journal*, August 16, 1991

68. Interview, November 18, 1992

69. Interview, February 22, 1993

70. Interview, November 18, 1992

71. Interview, December 14, 1992

72. *Modern Materials Handling*, August 1992

73. Ibid

74. Ibid

75. *Sport Trends*, June 1992

76. Interview, November 16, 1992

77. Ibid

78. *The Wall Street Journal*, May 14. 1993

79. *Los Angeles Times*, December 16, 1990

80. The Limited, Inc. 1990 Annual Report

81. "Partnering as a Focused Marketing Strategy," *California Management Review*, Spring 1991

82. Interview, February 22, 1993

83. *Los Angeles Times*, June 19, 1992

84. Bruce Horovitz, *Los Angeles Times*, March 17, 1993

85. Interview, November 20, 1992

86. Interview, December 6, 1993

87. "Partnering as a Focused Market Strategy," *California Management Review*, Spring 1991

88. *Business Week*, November 16, 1992

89. Interview, February 22, 1993
90. Interview, November 16, 1992

91. Interview, February 22, 1993

92. Interview, November 18, 1992

93. Jack Stack, "Feed the Hunger—Inspire Your Workers to Act Like Owners," *Success*, October 1992

94. Jane Applegate, *Los Angeles Times*, July 6, 1993

95. Interview, November 18, 1992

96. Ibid

97. Interview, December 14, 1992

98. Interview, November 11, 1992

99. *The Wall Street Journal*, September 24, 1993

100. Elton Mayo, *The Human Problems of an Industrial Civilization*, (New York: The MacMillan Company, 1933) and F.J. Roethlisberger, *Management and the Worker*, (Cambridge: Harvard University Press, 1946)

101. Amgen Inc. 1992 Annual Report

102. *Fortune*, April 6, 1992

103. Ibid

104. Lauren A. Leonardo, California Lutheran University, March 15, 1993

105. *Fortune*, June 17, 1991

106. Ibid

107. Ibid

108. Donnelly Corporation 1992 Annual Report

109. Herman Miller, Inc. 1992 Financial Statement

110. *MSU Business Topics*, Winter 1978

111. *New Management*, Spring 1986

112. Ibid

113. *Participative Management At Herman Miller*, Herman Miller Publications, 1992

114. Interview, November 18, 1992

115. Scanlon Plan Associates®, Lansing, Michigan

116. Interview, November 18, 1992

117. *New Management*, Spring 1996

118. Interview, December 31, 1992

119. James S. Hirsch, *The Wall Street Journal*, March 5, 1993

120. Interview, February 22, 1993

121. *Fortune*, June 17, 1991

122. Interview, November 18, 1992

123. *Industry Week*, October 21, 1991

124. Interview, May 6, 1993

125. Interview, December 31, 1992

126. *U.S. News & World Report*, August 2, 1993

127. Ibid

128. Ibid

129. Interview, December 14, 1992

130. Letter from Roger Tompkins, January 8, 1993

131. Interview, November 16, 1992

132. Telephone interview, December 1, 1993

133. *Organizational Behavior, 6th Edition*

134. Dr. Wayne W. Dyer, *The Sky's The Limit*, (Simon and Schuster: New York, 1980)

135. Interview November 18, 1992

136. Interview, December 14, 1992

INDEX

TO CONTACT THE AUTHOR

My sincere hope is that you'll adopt the *Partnering Paradigm*. Should you need additional assistance, I want you to be able to reach me. While my income is primary earned as a consultant, professional speaker, and author, I'm always willing to answer a quick question. If you call and I'm away, leave your number and I'll call you back collect. My AT&T Easy Reach number, is one that I plan to keep for life:

0-700-RIGSBEE (744-7233)

For those of you who are currently partnering and have a story to share, please drop me a line, I look forward to hearing from you. I'm especially interested in hearing about how you have successfully employed ideas from this book. Maybe your story—will some day end up in print.

I would be privileged to be the keynote speaker at your next company or association meeting. To assist you with your business challenges, my company also offers consulting services and customized training programs. If you've enjoyed the book, you'll enjoy working with us in developing solutions for your business challenges.

Rigsbee Enterprises, Inc.
P.O. Box 6425
Westlake Village, California 91359
Tel: (805) 371-4636   Fax: (805) 371-4631

Sincerely,
Edwin Richard Rigsbee